THE AUSTRALIAN
Women's Weekly
family favourites

acp books

CONTENTS

Buy the best flavoured
tomatoes you can find to
make the most of this salad.

CAPRESE SALAD WITH FIGS

preparation time 20 minutes | serves 4

4 large tomatoes (480g), sliced thinly
4 large fresh figs (320g), sliced thinly
25 cherry bocconcini cheeses (375g), drained, sliced thinly
½ small red onion (50g), chopped finely
¼ cup firmly packed fresh basil leaves
2 tablespoons olive oil
1 tablespoon balsamic vinegar

1 Overlap slices of tomato, fig and cheese on serving plate.
2 Sprinkle with onion and basil; drizzle with combined oil and vinegar.
nutritional count per serving 23.7g total fat (10.7g saturated fat); 1367kJ
(327 cal); 8.8g carbohydrate; 18.5g protein; 3.4g fibre

STARTERS

THAI BEEF SALAD WITH RICE VERMICELLI

preparation time 30 minutes | cooking time 15 minutes | serves 4

600g beef rump steak
250g rice vermicelli
2 lebanese cucumbers (260g),
   seeded, sliced thinly
250g cherry tomatoes, quartered
1 small red capsicum (150g),
   sliced thinly
1 small red onion (100g),
   sliced thinly
1 cup firmly packed fresh
   coriander leaves
1 cup firmly packed fresh
   mint leaves
sweet and sour dressing
½ cup (125ml) water
⅓ cup (75g) caster sugar
¼ cup (60ml) lime juice
1 tablespoon fish sauce
1 tablespoon light soy sauce
2 fresh small red thai chillies,
   chopped finely
1 clove garlic, crushed
1cm piece fresh ginger (5g), grated

1 Make sweet and sour dressing.
2 Cook beef on heated oiled grill plate (or grill or barbecue). Cover; stand 10 minutes, then slice thinly.
3 Meanwhile, place vermicelli in large heatproof bowl, cover with boiling water. Stand until tender; drain. Rinse vermicelli under cold water; drain. Using scissors, cut vermicelli into random lengths.
4 Combine beef and vermicelli in large bowl with remaining ingredients and dressing.
sweet and sour dressing Combine the water and sugar in small saucepan; stir over heat, without boiling, until sugar dissolves. Bring to the boil; boil, uncovered, without stirring, about 5 minutes or until syrup thickens slightly. Remove from heat; stir in remaining ingredients. Cool.
nutritional count per serving 5.1g total fat (1.7g saturated fat); 2057kJ (492 cal); 65.9g carbohydrate; 41.9g protein; 4.9g fibre

For a traditional-style thai beef salad, cook the beef rare – not only does the rare meat taste good, but the pinkish flesh looks stunning in the salad. Be sure to buy a good-quality piece of rump, to ensure your beef tastes its best. We like to serve the beef warm in this salad, but cold is fine, too.

Butter lettuce has small, round, loosely-formed heads with a sweet flavour; soft, buttery-textured leaves range from pale green on the outer leaves to pale yellow-green on the inner leaves. Good quality frozen crab meat is available from fishmongers.

PRAWN, CRAB AND AVOCADO SALAD

preparation time 25 minutes | serves 4

16 cooked medium king prawns
   (800g)
4 large butter lettuce leaves
250g crab meat, shredded coarsely
1 large avocado (320g),
   sliced thinly
thousand island dressing
½ cup (150g) mayonnaise
1 tablespoon tomato sauce
½ small red capsicum (75g),
   chopped finely
½ small white onion (40g),
   grated finely
8 pimiento-stuffed green olives,
   chopped finely
1 teaspoon lemon juice

1 Make thousand island dressing.
2 Shell and devein prawns, leaving tails intact.
3 Divide lettuce leaves among serving plates; divide prawns, crab and avocado among lettuce leaves. Drizzle with dressing.
thousand island dressing Combine ingredients in small bowl.
nutritional count per serving 26.5g total fat (4.4g saturated fat); 1718kJ (411 cal); 11.5g carbohydrate; 30.7g protein; 2.8g fibre

Greek salad is a great
accompaniment to beef
or lamb kebabs – perfect
for a summertime barbecue
or for dinner when you're
pressed for time.

GREEK SALAD

preparation time 20 minutes | serves 4

1 Whisk oil, juice, vinegar, oregano and garlic in large bowl; add
remaining ingredients, mix gently.
nutritional count per serving 25.8g total fat (9.6g saturated fat); 1359kJ
(325 cal); 10.8g carbohydrate; 11.5g protein; 3.2g fibre

¼ cup (60ml) olive oil
1 tablespoon lemon juice
1 tablespoon white wine vinegar
1 tablespoon finely chopped
   fresh oregano
1 clove garlic, crushed
3 medium tomatoes (450g),
   cut into wedges
2 lebanese cucumbers (260g),
   chopped coarsely
1 small red onion (100g),
   sliced thinly
1 small red capsicum (150g),
   sliced thinly
½ cup (75g) seeded black olives
200g fetta cheese, chopped coarsely

TUNA SALAD

preparation time 15 minutes | serves 4

1 Combine oil, vinegar, juice, herbs, garlic and chilli in screw-top jar; shake well.
2 Place lettuce wedges on serving plate; top with remaining ingredients. Drizzle with dressing.
nutritional count per serving 26.1g total fat (4.9g saturated fat); 1492kJ (357 cal); 4.6g carbohydrate; 24.4g protein; 4.9g fibre

¼ cup (60ml) olive oil
2 tablespoons white wine vinegar
1 tablespoon lemon juice
2 teaspoons finely chopped fresh basil
2 teaspoons finely chopped fresh oregano
1 clove garlic, crushed
1 fresh long red chilli, chopped finely
1 medium iceberg lettuce, cut into wedges
425g can tuna in springwater, drained, flaked
250g cherry tomatoes, halved
1 medium avocado (250g), chopped coarsely
1 lebanese cucumber (130g), sliced thinly
1 small red onion (100g), sliced thinly

Feel free to pick and choose any vegies to toss into this salad; capsicum and radish would taste great, too.
A can of salmon can be substituted for the tuna, if you prefer.

Perfect tabbouleh relies on perfect parsley: it's imperative that the parsley is well washed to remove any grit and dried thoroughly before adding to the salad. If the parsley is too wet, you will find that your tabbouleh turns a little mushy, rather than being light and tasty. Serve the tabbouleh with good-quality felafel.

TABBOULEH

preparation time 30 minutes (plus refrigeration time) | serves 4

¼ cup (40g) burghul
3 medium tomatoes (450g)
3 cups coarsely chopped fresh
   flat-leaf parsley
3 green onions, chopped finely
½ cup coarsely chopped
   fresh mint
1 clove garlic, crushed
¼ cup (60ml) lemon juice
¼ cup (60ml) olive oil

1 Place burghul in shallow medium bowl. Halve tomatoes, scoop pulp from tomato over burghul. Chop tomato flesh finely; spread over burghul. Cover; refrigerate 1 hour.
2 Combine burghul mixture in large bowl with remaining ingredients.
nutritional count per serving 14.2g total fat (2g saturated fat); 790kJ (189 cal); 9.4g carbohydrate; 3.6g protein; 5.9g fibre

Whether you're a big kid or a little kid, this salad is not just good for dinner, but lunch the next day, too; so double the recipe and you've got lunch covered for work the next day. Cornichon, French for gherkin, is a very small variety of pickled cucumber; it can be used in place of the dill pickles.

CREAMY CHICKEN AND PASTA SALAD

preparation time 20 minutes | cooking time 15 minutes | serves 6

1 Bring the water to the boil in medium saucepan, add chicken; simmer, covered, about 10 minutes. Cool chicken in poaching liquid 10 minutes; drain, slice thinly.
2 Meanwhile, cook pasta in large saucepan of boiling water until tender; drain. Rinse under cold water; drain.
3 Make creamy tarragon dressing.
4 Combine pasta in large bowl with chicken, dressing and remaining ingredients.
creamy tarragon dressing Combine ingredients in small bowl.
nutritional count per serving 39.1g total fat (8.8g saturated fat); 3097kJ (741 cal); 67.5g carbohydrate; 27.1g protein; 5.7g fibre

3 cups (750ml) water
400g chicken breast fillets
500g large pasta shells
2 trimmed celery stalks (200g), sliced thinly
1 small red onion (100g), sliced thinly
1 cup (120g) roasted pecans
½ cup (90g) thinly sliced dill pickles
50g baby rocket leaves
creamy tarragon dressing
¾ cup (225g) mayonnaise
½ cup (120g) sour cream
2 tablespoons lemon juice
1 tablespoon finely chopped fresh tarragon

CAESAR SALAD

preparation time 20 minutes | cooking time 10 minutes | serves 4

1 small french bread stick (150g)
¼ cup (60ml) olive oil
1 clove garlic, crushed
4 rindless bacon rashers (260g)
1 large cos lettuce, trimmed,
    chopped coarsely
3 green onions, sliced thinly
1 cup (80g) flaked parmesan cheese
4 hard-boiled eggs, quartered
caesar dressing
2 egg yolks
1 clove garlic, quartered
1 anchovy fillet
1 tablespoon lemon juice
1 tablespoon worcestershire sauce
2 teaspoons dijon mustard
½ cup (125ml) olive oil

1 Preheat oven to 180°C/160°C fan-forced.
2 Make caesar dressing.
3 Halve bread lengthways; slice halves thinly. Combine oil and garlic in large bowl with bread; place bread on oven tray. Toast bread in oven until croutons are brown.
4 Meanwhile, cook bacon in heated large frying pan until crisp; drain on absorbent paper. Chop bacon coarsely.
5 Combine lettuce, half the croutons, half the bacon, half the onion, half the cheese and half the dressing in large bowl.
6 Divide salad among serving bowls; top with egg and remaining ingredients. Drizzle with remaining dressing.
caesar dressing Blend or process egg yolks, garlic, anchovy, juice, sauce and mustard until smooth. With motor operating, gradually add oil in a thin, steady stream; process until mixture thickens. Stir in about a tablespoon of warm water to make dressing pourable.
nutritional count per serving 62.4g total fat (14g saturated fat); 3394kJ (812 cal); 25.4g carbohydrate; 36.2g protein; 5.7g fibre

Smoked salmon can replace the
bacon in this recipe; top salad with
about 50g salmon per person before
drizzling with the dressing.

In Italian, the word "ciabatta" means slipper, the traditional shape of this popular crisp-crusted, open-textured white sourdough bread. It is a good bread to use for bruschetta.

CREAMY PUMPKIN AND POTATO SOUP

preparation time 15 minutes | cooking time 20 minutes | serves 4

1 tablespoon olive oil
1 medium brown onion (150g),
    chopped coarsely
1 clove garlic, crushed
600g pumpkin, chopped coarsely
2 medium potatoes (400g),
    chopped coarsely
2 cups (500ml) water
1½ cups (375ml) vegetable stock
½ cup (125ml) cream
1 tablespoon lemon juice
garlic and chive croutons
⅓ loaf ciabatta (150g)
2 tablespoons olive oil
1 clove garlic, crushed
1 tablespoon finely chopped
    fresh chives

1 Heat oil in large saucepan; cook onion and garlic, stirring, until onion softens. Add pumpkin, potato, the water and stock; bring to the boil. Reduce heat; simmer, covered, about 20 minutes or until vegetables are tender.
2 Meanwhile, make garlic and chive croutons.
3 Blend or process soup, in batches, until smooth. Return soup to same pan; add cream and juice. Reheat, stirring, without boiling, until hot.
4 Serve bowls of soup topped with croutons.
garlic and chive croutons Preheat oven to 180°C/160°C fan-forced. Cut bread into 2cm cubes; combine bread in large bowl with oil, garlic and chives. Place bread on oven tray; toast bread in oven until croutons are brown.
nutritional count per serving 29.3g total fat (11.7g saturated fat); 2006kJ (480 cal); 41.4g carbohydrate; 10.7g protein; 5g fibre

Borlotti beans, also known as roman beans or pink beans, are available fresh or dried. They are interchangeable with pinto beans because of the similarity in appearance – both are pale pink or beige with dark red streaks. If you don't have any dried beans, you can add a can of rinsed, drained beans of your choice at the end of step 3 and stir until heated through; reduce the cooking time by 1 hour in step 2.

MINESTRONE

preparation time 30 minutes (plus standing time) | cooking time 2 hours | serves 6

1 Place borlotti beans in medium bowl, cover with water; stand overnight, drain. Rinse under cold water; drain.
2 Heat oil in large saucepan; cook onion and garlic, stirring, until onion softens. Add paste; cook, stirring, 2 minutes. Add borlotti beans to pan with the water, stock and pasta sauce; bring to the boil. Reduce heat; simmer, uncovered, about 1 hour or until beans are tender.
3 Add celery; simmer, uncovered, 10 minutes. Add carrot, zucchini and green beans; simmer, uncovered, about 20 minutes or until carrot is tender. Add pasta; simmer until pasta is tender.
4 Serve bowls of soup sprinkled with basil.
nutritional count per serving 5.5g total fat (1g saturated fat); 1095kJ (262 cal); 39.9g carbohydrate; 9.4g protein; 6.5g fibre

1 cup (200g) dried borlotti beans
1 tablespoon olive oil
1 medium brown onion (150g), chopped coarsely
1 clove garlic, crushed
¼ cup (70g) tomato paste
1.5 litres (6 cups) water
2 cups (500ml) vegetable stock
700g bottled tomato pasta sauce
1 trimmed celery stalk (100g), chopped finely
1 medium carrot (120g), chopped finely
1 medium zucchini (120g), chopped finely
80g green beans, trimmed, chopped finely
¾ cup (135g) macaroni
⅓ cup coarsely chopped fresh basil

CHICKEN WONTON SOUP

preparation time 40 minutes (plus refrigeration time) | cooking time 2 hours 20 minutes | serves 4

1 tablespoon olive oil
1 medium brown onion (150g),
    chopped coarsely
1 clove garlic, sliced thinly
2cm piece fresh ginger (10g),
    sliced thinly
1.5 litres (6 cups) water
2 cups (500ml) chicken stock
1kg chicken bones
1 medium carrot (120g),
    chopped coarsely
1 trimmed celery stalk (100g),
    chopped coarsely
1 tablespoon light soy sauce
4 green onions, sliced thinly
chicken wontons
150g chicken mince
1 fresh small red thai chilli,
    chopped finely
1 clove garlic, crushed
1cm piece fresh ginger (5g), grated
2 teaspoons light soy sauce
1 green onion, sliced thinly
16 x 8cm round wonton wrappers

1 Heat oil in large saucepan; cook brown onion, garlic and ginger, stirring, until onion softens. Add the water, stock, bones, carrot and celery; bring to the boil. Reduce heat; simmer, covered, 2 hours.
2 Strain broth through muslin-lined sieve or colander into large heatproof bowl; discard solids. Cool; cover, refrigerate overnight.
3 Make chicken wontons.
4 Skim and discard fat from surface of broth. Return broth to large saucepan with sauce; bring to the boil. Add wontons, reduce heat; cook about 5 minutes.
5 Divide wontons among bowls; ladle broth into bowls and sprinkle with green onion.
chicken wontons Combine chicken, chilli, garlic, ginger, sauce and onion in small bowl. Place a rounded teaspoon of chicken mixture in centre of each wonton wrapper; brush around edges with a little water, gather edges around filling, pinch together to seal.
nutritional count per serving 5.5g total fat (2g saturated fat); 560kJ (134 cal); 4.7g carbohydrate; 16.6g protein; 0.2g fibre

Double the recipe for the chicken wontons and pop one batch, sealed tightly, in the freezer. Wontons make a yummy party nibble and, best of all, require very little effort to cook – all you need do is steam them in a baking-paper-lined bamboo steamer set over a large pan of simmering water until the chicken is cooked. Serve them with soy sauce for dipping.

For an added vegie kick, toss a coarsely chopped trimmed bunch of spinach into the soup when you add the corn and peas.

CHUNKY BEEF AND VEGETABLE SOUP

preparation time 20 minutes | cooking time 2 hours | serves 4

2 tablespoons olive oil
600g gravy beef, trimmed,
    cut into 2cm pieces
1 medium brown onion (150g),
    chopped coarsely
1 clove garlic, crushed
1.5 litres (6 cups) water
1 cup (250ml) beef stock
400g can diced tomatoes
2 trimmed celery stalks (200g),
    cut into 1cm pieces
1 medium carrot (120g),
    cut into 1cm pieces
2 small potatoes (240g),
    cut into 1cm pieces
310g can corn kernels,
    rinsed, drained
½ cup (60g) frozen peas

1 Heat half the oil in large saucepan; cook beef, in batches, until browned.
2 Heat remaining oil in same pan; cook onion and garlic, stirring, until onion softens. Return beef to pan with the water, stock and undrained tomatoes; bring to the boil. Reduce heat; simmer, covered, 1½ hours.
3 Add celery, carrot and potato to soup; simmer, uncovered, about 20 minutes or until vegetables are tender.
4 Add corn and peas to soup; stir over heat until peas are tender.
nutritional count per serving 17g total fat (4.3g saturated fat); 1768kJ (423 cal); 26.7g carbohydrate; 36.9g protein; 7.5g fibre

You could also use chicken mince instead of the pork and veal mince. The mince mixture can be served in witlof or betel leaves, for impressive cocktail food.

PORK AND VEAL SANG CHOY BOW

preparation time 20 minutes | cooking time 20 minutes | serves 4

1 Heat oil in wok; stir-fry mince, ginger and garlic until mince browns.
2 Add mushrooms and water chestnut; stir-fry until vegetables are tender. Add sauces and juice; stir-fry until hot. Remove from heat; stir in sprouts.
3 Divide mince mixture among lettuce leaves; sprinkle with onion.
nutritional count per serving 16.1g total fat (5g saturated fat); 1363kJ (326 cal); 9.6g carbohydrate; 33.7g protein; 4.1g fibre

1 tablespoon peanut oil
600g pork and veal mince
2cm piece fresh ginger (10g), grated
2 cloves garlic, crushed
50g fresh shiitake mushrooms, chopped finely
227g can water chestnuts, rinsed, drained, chopped finely
2 tablespoons char siu sauce
1 tablespoon oyster sauce
1 tablespoon light soy sauce
1 tablespoon lime juice
1 cup (80g) bean sprouts
8 large iceberg lettuce leaves
2 green onions, sliced thinly

We used a sweet-chilli-flavoured tofu in this recipe, available already marinated. Various-flavoured marinated tofu pieces can be found, cryovac-packed, in the refrigerated section in most supermarkets and Asian food stores.

PRAWN AND SCALLOP LAKSA

preparation time 45 minutes | cooking time 30 minutes | serves 6

1 Shell and devein prawns, leaving tails intact.

2 Make laksa paste.

3 Cook paste in large saucepan, stirring, about 5 minutes or until fragrant. Stir in stock, coconut milk and lime leaves; bring to the boil. Reduce heat; simmer, covered, 20 minutes.

4 Meanwhile, place noodles in large heatproof bowl, cover with boiling water; stand until tender, drain.

5 Add prawns to laksa mixture; simmer, uncovered, about 5 minutes or until prawns change colour. Add scallops and tofu; simmer, uncovered, about 3 minutes or until scallops change colour. Remove from heat; stir in juice.

6 Divide noodles among serving bowls; ladle laksa into bowls, top with sprouts, onion, chilli and coriander.

laksa paste Cover chillies with the water in small heatproof bowl, stand 10 minutes; drain. Blend or process chillies with remaining ingredients until smooth.

nutritional count per serving 35.4g total fat (25.9g saturated fat); 2207kJ (528 cal); 25.1g carbohydrate; 25.7g protein; 5g fibre

12 uncooked medium king prawns (540g)
1 litre (4 cups) chicken stock
3¼ cups (810ml) coconut milk
4 kaffir lime leaves, shredded finely
150g rice stick noodles
300g scallops, roe removed
150g marinated tofu, cut into 2cm pieces
2 tablespoons lime juice
2 cups (160g) bean sprouts
4 green onions, sliced thinly
1 fresh long red chilli, sliced thinly
½ cup loosely packed fresh coriander leaves

laksa paste
3 medium dried chillies
⅓ cup (80ml) boiling water
2 teaspoons peanut oil
1 small brown onion (80g), chopped coarsely
2 cloves garlic, quartered
2cm piece fresh ginger (10g), grated
10cm stick fresh lemon grass (20g), chopped finely
1 tablespoon halved unroasted, unsalted macadamias
1 tablespoon coarsely chopped fresh coriander root and stem mixture
½ teaspoon ground turmeric
½ teaspoon ground coriander
¼ cup loosely packed fresh mint leaves

Salt and pepper prawns taste delicious, too. Shell and devein the prawns, leaving tails intact, and dip into the salt and pepper mix. Like squid, prawns take no time to cook, making them a great dish to serve as a starter. For a more substantial meal, serve with the Greek Salad on page 9.

SALT AND PEPPER SQUID WITH AÏOLI

preparation time 30 minutes | cooking time 15 minutes | serves 4

600g squid hoods, cleaned
¼ cup (35g) plain flour
1½ teaspoons sea salt flakes
1½ teaspoons cracked black pepper
1 teaspoon dried chilli flakes
vegetable oil, for deep-frying
40g baby rocket leaves
1 large tomato (220g), seeded, chopped finely
lemon aïoli
2 egg yolks
1 teaspoon dijon mustard
⅔ cup (160ml) extra light olive oil
⅓ cup (80ml) olive oil
2 tablespoons lemon juice
2 cloves garlic, crushed

1 Make lemon aïoli.
2 Cut squid down centre to open out; score the inside in a diagonal pattern. Halve squid lengthways; slice halves crossways into thick strips.
3 Combine flour, salt, pepper and chilli in medium bowl; add squid, toss to coat in flour mixture. Shake off excess.
4 Heat oil in wok; deep-fry squid, in batches, until tender, drain.
5 Serve squid with rocket, tomato and aïoli.
lemon aïoli Whisk egg yolks and mustard in medium bowl. Gradually whisk in combined oils, in a thin, steady stream until mixture thickens. Stir in juice and garlic.
nutritional count per serving 67.1g total fat (10.1g saturated fat); 3118kJ (746 cal); 8.2g carbohydrate; 28.6g protein; 1.6g fibre

Serve the chicken wings with the Vegetable and Omelette Fried Rice on page 91 for a kid-friendly dinner. The chicken wings are also a perfect, inexpensive party snack for young and old alike.

HONEY, SOY AND SESAME CHICKEN WINGS

preparation time 15 minutes (plus refrigeration time) | cooking time 30 minutes | serves 4

1kg chicken wings
¼ cup (60ml) japanese soy sauce
2 tablespoons honey
1 clove garlic, crushed
2cm piece fresh ginger (10g), grated
2 teaspoons sesame seeds
1 teaspoon sesame oil
2 green onions, sliced thinly

1 Cut chicken wings into three pieces at joints; discard tips. Combine sauce, honey, garlic, ginger, seeds and oil in large bowl with chicken. Cover; refrigerate 3 hours or overnight.
2 Preheat oven to 220°C/200°C fan-forced.
3 Place chicken, in single layer, on oiled wire rack over shallow large baking dish; brush remaining marinade over chicken. Roast about 30 minutes or until chicken is cooked.
4 Serve chicken wings sprinkled with onion.
nutritional count per serving 10.3g total fat (3g saturated fat); 1233kJ (295 cal); 12.6g carbohydrate; 37.4g protein; 0.4g fibre

BEEF BURRITO BASKETS

preparation time 40 minutes | cooking time 1 hour 15 minutes | serves 4

cooking-oil spray
4 x 15cm flour tortillas
2 tablespoons olive oil
600g beef rump steak,
    sliced thinly
1 medium brown onion (150g),
    chopped coarsely
1 small green capsicum (150g),
    sliced thinly
1 small yellow capsicum (150g),
    sliced thinly
1 clove garlic, crushed
1 teaspoon ground cumin
½ teaspoon ground coriander
¼ teaspoon ground cayenne pepper
400g can diced tomatoes
1½ cups (375ml) beef stock
1 tablespoon coarsely chopped
    fresh oregano
400g can kidney beans,
    rinsed, drained
1 cup (120g) coarsely grated
    cheddar cheese
⅓ cup (80g) sour cream
⅓ cup loosely packed fresh
    coriander leaves
avocado salsa
1 medium avocado (250g),
    chopped finely
1 medium tomato (150g),
    seeded, chopped finely
½ small red onion (50g),
    chopped finely
1 tablespoon lime juice
1 tablespoon olive oil

1 Preheat oven to 180°C/160°C fan-forced. Spray four holes of six-hole (¾-cup/180ml) texas muffin pan with oil.
2 Push tortillas carefully into pan holes; bake about 15 minutes or until crisp. Cool in pan.
3 Heat half the oil in large frying pan; cook beef, in batches, over high heat, until browned.
4 Heat remaining oil in same pan; cook onion, capsicums, garlic and spices, stirring, until onion softens. Return beef to pan with undrained tomatoes, stock and oregano; simmer, uncovered, about 1 hour or until sauce thickens and is reduced by half. Add beans; stir until heated through.
5 Meanwhile, make avocado salsa.
6 Divide beef mixture among tortilla cups; top with cheese. Bake about 5 minutes or until cheese melts.
7 Serve burrito baskets topped with sour cream, avocado salsa and coriander.
avocado salsa Combine ingredients in small bowl.
nutritional count per serving 54.9g total fat (20.7g saturated fat); 3507kJ (839 cal); 30.1g carbohydrate; 52.9g protein; 8.8g fibre

If you're after a shortcut, you can skip making the tortilla baskets in steps 1 and 2, and simply serve the beef mixture, avocado salsa and accompaniments in warmed tortillas.

You can use any combination of mushrooms in this recipe. Spring rolls can be frozen, uncooked, for up to three months. Thaw overnight in the refrigerator before cooking.

DUCK AND MUSHROOM SPRING ROLLS

preparation time 30 minutes | cooking time 20 minutes | makes 12

½ chinese barbecued duck (500g)
50g fresh shiitake mushrooms,
    sliced thinly
50g oyster mushrooms,
    sliced thinly
50g enoki mushrooms, trimmed
4 green onions, sliced thinly
1 clove garlic, crushed
2cm piece fresh ginger (10g),
    grated
1 tablespoon hoisin sauce
1 tablespoon lime juice
12 x 21.5cm-square spring roll
    wrappers
vegetable oil, for deep-frying

1 Remove skin and meat from duck; discard bones. Shred meat and skin finely.
2 Combine duck, mushrooms, onion, garlic, ginger, sauce and juice in medium bowl.
3 To assemble rolls, place one wrapper on board, with one corner of the wrapper facing you. Place a little of the duck filling onto corner; roll once toward opposing corner to cover filling, then fold in two remaining corners to enclose filling. Continue rolling; brush seam with a little water to seal spring roll. Repeat process with remaining wrappers and duck filling.
4 Heat oil in wok; deep-fry spring rolls, in batches, until browned lightly. Drain on absorbent paper.
5 Serve rolls with sweet chilli sauce, if you like.
nutritional count per serving 9.6g total fat (2.3g saturated fat); 585kJ (140 cal); 6.8g carbohydrate; 6.3g protein; 1.1g fibre

You can replace the chicken mince with the same quantity of pork or beef mince.

CHICKEN SAUSAGE ROLLS

preparation time 15 minutes | cooking time 30 minutes | makes 60

1 Preheat oven to 220°C/200°C fan-forced. Line oven trays with baking paper.
2 Combine mince, onion, breadcrumbs, egg, basil, semi-dried tomato and paste in large bowl.
3 Cut pastry sheets in half lengthways. Place equal amounts of chicken filling mixture lengthways along centre of each pastry piece; roll pastry to enclose filling. Cut each roll into six pieces; place rolls, seam-side down, on trays. Brush with extra egg; bake about 30 minutes.
4 Serve rolls hot, with tomato sauce.
nutritional count per serving 4.8g total fat (2.2g saturated fat); 359kJ (86 cal); 6g carbohydrate; 4.5g protein; 0.5g fibre

1kg chicken mince
1 medium brown onion (150g), chopped finely
½ cup (35g) stale breadcrumbs
1 egg
¼ cup finely chopped fresh basil
½ cup (75g) drained semi-dried tomatoes in oil, chopped finely
2 tablespoons tomato paste
5 sheets ready-rolled puff pastry
1 egg, extra

BARBECUED PORK RICE PAPER ROLLS

preparation time 30 minutes | makes 12

1 Combine pork, wombok, carrot, capsicum, sprouts, onion, mint, sauces and juice in large bowl.
2 To assemble rolls, place one rice paper sheet in medium bowl of warm water until softened. Lift sheet carefully from water; place, with one corner of the sheet facing you, on board covered with a tea towel. Place a little of the pork filling vertically along centre of sheet; fold top and bottom corners over filling then roll sheet from side to side to enclose filling. Repeat with remaining rice paper sheets and pork filling.
3 Make plum dipping sauce; serve with rolls.
plum dipping sauce Combine ingredients in small bowl.
nutritional count per serving 5.5g total fat (2.2g saturated fat); 548kJ (131 cal); 10.2g carbohydrate; 8.9g protein; 2.5g fibre

400g chinese barbecued pork,
    sliced thinly
½ small wombok (350g),
    shredded finely
1 small carrot (70g), grated coarsely
1 small red capsicum (150g),
    sliced thinly
1 cup (80g) bean sprouts
3 green onions, sliced thinly
½ cup loosely packed fresh
    mint leaves
1 tablespoon plum sauce
1 tablespoon sweet chilli sauce
1 tablespoon lime juice
12 x 17cm-square rice paper sheets
plum dipping sauce
2 tablespoons plum sauce
2 tablespoons sweet chilli sauce
2 tablespoons water
1 tablespoon lime juice
1 tablespoon light soy sauce

Chinese barbecued pork, a roasted pork fillet with a sweet, sticky coating, is available from Asian supermarkets. For a vegetarian version replace the pork with the same weight of firm tofu.

Serve the curry with steamed rice and naan bread for a delicious meal. You can buy naan bread from the bread section of most supermarkets.

PUMPKIN AND EGGPLANT CURRY

preparation time 20 minutes | cooking time 40 minutes | serves 6

2 tablespoons olive oil
1 medium brown onion (150g), sliced thickly
1 clove garlic, crushed
2cm piece fresh ginger (10g), grated
2 fresh small red thai chillies, chopped finely
1 teaspoon ground cumin
½ teaspoon ground turmeric
¼ teaspoon ground cardamom
¼ teaspoon ground fennel
8 baby eggplants (480g), sliced thickly
1kg butternut pumpkin, cut into 2cm pieces
400g can diced tomatoes
400ml can coconut cream
1 cup (250ml) vegetable stock
1 tablespoon tomato paste
400g can chickpeas, rinsed, drained
½ cup coarsely chopped fresh mint

1 Heat oil in large saucepan; cook onion, garlic, ginger and chilli, stirring, until onion softens. Add spices and eggplant; cook, stirring, 2 minutes.
2 Add pumpkin, undrained tomatoes, coconut cream, stock and paste; bring to the boil. Reduce heat; simmer, uncovered, 20 minutes. Add chickpeas; simmer, uncovered, about 10 minutes or until vegetables are tender.
3 Serve bowls of curry sprinkled with mint.
nutritional count per serving 22.3g total fat (13.6g saturated fat); 1467kJ (351 cal); 24.5g carbohydrate; 9.5g protein; 8.6g fibre

SUNDAY LUNCH

OSSO BUCO MILANESE

preparation time 30 minutes | cooking time 2 hours 30 minutes | serves 6

12 pieces veal osso buco (3.5kg)
¼ cup (35g) plain flour
¼ cup (60ml) olive oil
1 medium brown onion (150g),
    sliced thinly
2 cloves garlic, crushed
4 slices pancetta (60g),
    chopped coarsely
1 cup (250ml) dry white wine
2½ cups (625ml) chicken stock
¼ cup coarsely chopped fresh sage
1 bay leaf
pinch saffron threads
8 drained, marinated, quartered
    artichoke hearts (100g)
2 teaspoons finely grated
    lemon rind
2 tablespoons lemon juice

1 Coat veal in flour; shake off excess. Heat 2 tablespoons of the oil in large saucepan; cook veal, in batches, until browned all over.
2 Heat remaining oil in same pan; cook onion, garlic and pancetta, stirring, until onion softens. Stir in wine, stock, sage, bay leaf and saffron.
3 Return veal to pan, fitting pieces upright and tightly together in a single layer; bring to the boil. Reduce heat; simmer, covered, 1½ hours. Stir in artichokes; simmer, uncovered, 30 minutes.
4 Remove veal from pan; cover to keep warm. Bring sauce to the boil; boil, uncovered, about 10 minutes or until sauce thickens slightly. Stir in rind and juice.
5 Divide veal among serving plates; top with sauce. You can sprinkle with extra finely grated lemon rind and fresh sage leaves.
nutritional count per serving 12.1g total fat (2.2g saturated fat); 2136kJ (511 cal); 7.1g carbohydrate; 85.6g protein; 0.8g fibre

Veal osso buco is another name that butchers use for veal shin, usually cut into 3cm to 5cm thick slices.
Serve osso buco with creamy polenta for a comforting winter meal – all you need to do is combine 2 cups of milk and 2 cups of water in a large saucepan and bring to the boil. Gradually stir in 1 cup of polenta. Reduce the heat and simmer, stirring, about 5 minutes or until the polenta thickens. Stir in ½ cup finely grated parmesan cheese and ⅓ cup hot milk to finish.

Fresh pasta is available from the refrigerated section of most supermarkets. You can use dried pasta instead of fresh, however, you will need to cook the lasagne for at least half an hour longer.

BEEF AND EGGPLANT PARMIGIANA LASAGNE

preparation time 40 minutes | cooking time 2 hours 10 minutes | serves 8

1 tablespoon olive oil
1 medium brown onion (150g), chopped finely
1 clove garlic, crushed
1kg beef mince
½ cup (125ml) dry red wine
2 cups (500ml) beef stock
700g bottled tomato pasta sauce
¼ cup (70g) tomato paste
¾ cup finely chopped fresh basil
2 medium eggplants (600g), peeled, sliced thinly
cooking-oil spray
3 fresh lasagne sheets (150g)
2 cups (200g) coarsely grated mozzarella cheese
1 cup (100g) packaged breadcrumbs
½ cup (40g) coarsely grated parmesan cheese

1 Preheat oven to 200°C/180°C fan-forced.
2 Heat oil in large frying pan; cook onion and garlic, stirring, until onion softens. Add beef; cook, stirring, until browned. Add wine, stock, sauce and paste; bring to the boil. Reduce heat; simmer, covered, 30 minutes, stirring occasionally. Uncover; simmer about 30 minutes or until thickened slightly; stir in basil.
3 Meanwhile, place eggplant on oiled oven tray; spray with oil. Roast about 20 minutes or until tender.
4 Oil shallow 2.5-litre (10-cup) ovenproof dish. Cover base with lasagne sheets, cut to fit; top with about a third of the warm beef mixture, half the eggplant and ⅓ cup mozzarella cheese.
5 Repeat layering with remaining trimmed lasagne sheets, another third of the beef mixture, remaining eggplant and ⅓ cup mozzarella cheese. Finish with lasagne sheet. Spread remaining third of the beef mixture over lasagne; top with breadcrumbs, parmesan cheese and remaining mozzarella cheese. Bake, covered, 40 minutes.
6 Preheat grill.
7 Uncover lasagne; place under grill until browned lightly. Stand 5 minutes before serving.
nutritional count per serving 20.9g total fat (8.9g saturated fat); 2123kJ (508 cal); 33.6g carbohydrate; 41g protein; 5.2g fibre

This recipe can be made in a 2-litre (8-cup) ovenproof dish, rather than individual dishes, if you prefer.

VEAL GOULASH AND POTATO PIES

preparation time 25 minutes | cooking time 2 hours | serves 6

1 Heat 1 tablespoon of the oil in large saucepan; cook veal, in batches, until browned.
2 Heat remaining oil in same pan; cook onion, capsicum and garlic, stirring, until onion softens. Add flour, spices and seeds; cook, stirring, 2 minutes.
3 Return veal to pan with stock, undrained tomatoes and paste; bring to the boil. Reduce heat; simmer, covered, 1 hour. Uncover; simmer about 30 minutes or until veal is tender and sauce thickens slightly.
4 Meanwhile, boil, steam or microwave potato until tender; drain. Mash potato in medium bowl until smooth.
5 Preheat grill.
6 Divide goulash mixture among six oiled 1¼-cup (310ml) ovenproof dishes; top with potato, sprinkle with cheese. Grill until browned.
nutritional count per serving 20.6g total fat (6.8g saturated fat); 2011kJ (481 cal); 23g carbohydrate; 48.8g protein; 3.9g fibre

¼ cup (60ml) olive oil
1kg boneless veal shoulder,
  cut into 2cm pieces
1 large brown onion (200g),
  chopped coarsely
1 large red capsicum (350g),
  chopped coarsely
1 clove garlic, crushed
1 tablespoon plain flour
2 teaspoons hot paprika
2 teaspoons sweet paprika
2 teaspoons caraway seeds
2 cups (500ml) beef stock
400g can diced tomatoes
1 tablespoon tomato paste
4 medium potatoes (800g),
  chopped coarsely
1 cup (120g) coarsely grated
  cheddar cheese

A simple garden salad would make a great addition to this meal. Any combination of herbs can be used in the stuffing, so feel free to add any of your favourite herbs from your herb garden.

SIRLOIN ROAST WITH POTATO AND KUMARA WEDGES

preparation time 35 minutes | cooking time 1 hour 50 minutes | serves 8

1 Make cheese and herb stuffing.

2 Preheat oven to 220°C/200°C fan-forced.

3 Cut between fat and meat of beef, making a pocket for stuffing; trim and discard a little of the fat. Spoon stuffing into pocket; lay fat over stuffing to enclose. Tie beef with kitchen string at 2cm intervals; place beef on wire rack over shallow large baking dish.

4 Roast, uncovered, about 1½ hours.

5 Meanwhile, cut kumara into thirds crossways; cut each piece into wedges. Combine kumara with potato, oil, juice, paprika and garlic in shallow large baking dish; roast about 1 hour.

6 Remove beef from dish; cover, stand 10 minutes. Slice beef thinly.

7 Reserve 2 tablespoons of beef juices in baking dish; place over heat. Add flour; cook, stirring, until mixture thickens and bubbles. Gradually add wine and stock, stirring, until gravy boils and thickens slightly.

8 Serve beef with potato and kumara wedges and gravy.

cheese and herb stuffing Melt butter in medium frying pan; cook bacon, onion and garlic, stirring, until onion softens. Cool. Combine bacon mixture with remaining ingredients in medium bowl.

nutritional count per serving 43.5g total fat (19g saturated fat); 3716kJ (889 cal); 41.6g carbohydrate; 78.7g protein; 4.8g fibre

2.5kg boneless beef sirloin roast
2 large kumara (1kg)
1kg potatoes, cut into wedges
2 tablespoons olive oil
2 tablespoons lemon juice
2 teaspoons sweet paprika
1 clove garlic, crushed
2 tablespoons plain flour
⅓ cup (80ml) dry red wine
1½ cups (375ml) beef stock

cheese and herb stuffing
50g butter
2 rashers rindless bacon (130g), chopped finely
1 medium brown onion (150g), chopped finely
1 clove garlic, crushed
1½ cups (105g) stale breadcrumbs
½ cup (40g) coarsely grated parmesan cheese
1 egg
1 tablespoon wholegrain mustard
2 tablespoons finely chopped fresh oregano
2 tablespoons finely chopped fresh flat-leaf parsley
2 teaspoons finely grated lemon rind

CHUNKY BEEF AND VEGETABLE PIE

preparation time 40 minutes | cooking time 2 hours | serves 8

1 tablespoon olive oil

1.5kg gravy beef,
cut into 2cm pieces

60g butter

1 medium brown onion (150g),
chopped finely

1 clove garlic, crushed

¼ cup (35g) plain flour

1 cup (250ml) dry white wine

3 cups (750ml) hot beef stock

2 tablespoons tomato paste

2 trimmed celery stalks (200g),
cut into 2cm pieces

2 medium potatoes (400g),
cut into 2cm pieces

1 large carrot (180g),
cut into 2cm pieces

1 large zucchini (150g),
cut into 2cm pieces

150g mushrooms, quartered

1 cup (120g) frozen peas

½ cup finely chopped fresh
flat-leaf parsley

2 sheets ready-rolled puff pastry

1 egg, beaten lightly

1 Heat oil in large saucepan; cook beef, in batches, until browned all over.

2 Melt butter in same pan; cook onion and garlic, stirring, until onion softens. Add flour; cook, stirring, until mixture thickens and bubbles. Gradually stir in wine and stock; stir until mixture boils and thickens slightly.

3 Return beef to pan with paste, celery, potato and carrot; bring to the boil. Reduce heat; simmer, covered, 1 hour.

4 Add zucchini and mushrooms; simmer, uncovered, about 30 minutes or until beef is tender. Add peas; stir until heated through. Remove from heat; stir in parsley.

5 Preheat oven to 220°C/200°C fan-forced.

6 Divide warm beef mixture between two deep 25cm pie dishes; brush outside edge of dishes with a little egg. Top each pie with a pastry sheet; pressing edges to seal. Trim pastry; brush pastry with egg.

7 Bake about 20 minutes or until browned.

nutritional count per serving 27.6g total fat (13.3g saturated fat); 2412kJ (577 cal); 28.6g carbohydrate; 46.4g protein; 4.9g fibre

If you only need to serve four, you can either
halve the recipe, or freeze the second pie,
cooked or uncooked, for up to three months.

We've made our own pesto for this recipe, however, if you're pressed for time, you can replace it with a ready-made pesto of your choice; sun-dried-tomato pesto would taste great in this recipe, too.

PICNIC COTTAGE LOAF

preparation time 40 minutes (plus refrigeration time) | cooking time 25 minutes | serves 6

1 Make rocket pesto.

2 Preheat oven to 220°C/200°C fan-forced.

3 Quarter capsicum; discard seeds and membranes. Roast or grill, skin-side up, until skin blisters and blackens. Cover capsicum pieces with plastic or paper for 5 minutes; peel away skin.

4 Place zucchini and eggplant on oiled oven tray; spray with oil. Roast about 15 minutes; cool.

5 Meanwhile, heat oil in medium frying pan; cook onion, stirring, until soft. Add sugar and vinegar; cook, stirring, until onion caramelises.

6 Cut shallow lid from top of loaf; remove soft bread inside, leaving 2cm-thick shell.

7 Spread pesto inside bread shell and lid. Layer eggplant, cheese, onion mixture, zucchini, capsicum, beef and rocket inside bread shell, pressing layers down firmly. Replace lid; press down firmly.

8 Wrap loaf tightly with kitchen string and plastic wrap; refrigerate about 2 hours or until required.

rocket pesto Blend or process rocket, nuts, cheese, garlic and juice until coarsely chopped. With motor operating, gradually add oil in a thin steady stream; process until thick.

nutritional count per serving 24g total fat (6.2g saturated fat); 2069kJ (495 cal); 43.1g carbohydrate; 23.8g protein; 5.4g fibre

1 large red capsicum (350g)
1 large zucchini (150g), sliced thinly lengthways
1 medium eggplant (300g), sliced thinly
cooking-oil spray
1 tablespoon olive oil
1 large red onion (300g), sliced thinly
1 tablespoon brown sugar
1 tablespoon red wine vinegar
1 round cob loaf (450g)
1 cup (240g) ricotta cheese
200g thinly sliced rare roast beef
20g baby rocket leaves

rocket pesto
20g baby rocket leaves
¼ cup (40g) roasted pine nuts
¼ cup (20g) coarsely grated parmesan cheese
1 clove garlic, quartered
1 tablespoon lemon juice
2 tablespoons olive oil

Broad beans are available both frozen and fresh from most supermarkets. If you can't find any, you can use frozen peas in the mash, instead.

LAMB LEG ROAST WITH BROAD BEAN MASH

preparation time 30 minutes (plus refrigeration time) | cooking time 1 hour 20 minutes | serves 6

2kg lamb leg
2 tablespoons olive oil
2 cloves garlic, crushed
1 tablespoon wholegrain mustard
2 teaspoons finely grated
    lemon rind
1 tablespoon lemon juice
1.5kg potatoes, chopped coarsely
2 cups (240g) peeled broad beans
40g butter
¾ cup (180ml) hot milk
mint sauce
2 cups firmly packed fresh
    mint leaves
2 cloves garlic, quartered
½ cup (125ml) olive oil
¼ cup (60ml) white wine vinegar
1 tablespoon caster sugar

1 Using sharp knife, score lamb skin at 2cm intervals. Combine lamb, oil, garlic, mustard, rind and juice in large bowl. Cover; refrigerate 3 hours or overnight.
2 Preheat oven to 200°C/180°C fan-forced.
3 Place lamb on oiled wire rack over large baking dish; roast about 45 minutes. Cover lamb; stand 10 minutes, slice thinly.
4 Meanwhile, boil, steam or microwave potato and beans, separately, until tender; drain. Push potato through fine sieve into large bowl; stir in butter and milk until smooth. Place beans in small bowl; crush coarsely with fork. Fold beans into potato mixture.
5 Make mint sauce.
6 Serve lamb with mint sauce and broad bean mash.
mint sauce Blend or process mint and garlic until smooth; with motor operating, gradually add oil, in a thin steady stream, until mixture is smooth. Stir in vinegar and sugar.
nutritional count per serving 45.7g total fat (13.9g saturated fat); 3373kJ (807 cal); 32.6g carbohydrate; 63.6g protein; 6.4g fibre

Roast some potatoes with the chicken for the last hour of its cooking time – simply halve, spray with cooking oil and place around the chicken on the wire rack. Serve chicken with lemon wedges, if you like.

CRISPY-SKINNED ROAST CHICKEN WITH TOMATO BRAISED BEANS

preparation time 30 minutes | cooking time 2 hours 10 minutes | serves 6

1 Preheat oven to 200°C/180°C fan-forced.
2 Tuck wing tips under chicken. Fill cavity with lemon, thyme sprigs and garlic, fold skin over to enclose filling; secure with toothpicks. Tie legs together with kitchen string.
3 Combine butter, juice, crushed garlic and chopped thyme in small bowl; rub butter mixture all over chicken.
4 Place chicken on oiled rack in large baking dish; pour the water into dish. Roast about 2 hours, basting occasionally with pan juices.
5 Meanwhile, heat oil in large saucepan; cook onion, stirring, until onion softens. Add beans and tomato; cook, covered, stirring occasionally, about 20 minutes or until vegetables soften slightly.
6 Serve chicken with beans.
nutritional count per serving 33.5g total fat (12.7g saturated fat); 2123kJ (508 cal); 8.3g carbohydrate; 40.3g protein; 7.3g fibre

2kg chicken
1 medium lemon (140g), quartered
6 sprigs fresh thyme
6 cloves garlic, unpeeled
60g butter, softened
2 tablespoons lemon juice
2 cloves garlic, crushed
2 teaspoons finely chopped
    fresh thyme
1 cup (250ml) water
1 tablespoon olive oil
1 medium brown onion (150g),
    chopped coarsely
1kg green beans, trimmed
4 medium tomatoes (600g),
    chopped coarsely

American-style pork ribs are well-trimmed mid-loin ribs; you will find them at butcher shops and most supermarkets.

SATAY PORK RIBS WITH COLESLAW

preparation time 35 minutes (plus refrigeration time) | cooking time 1 hour | serves 8

3kg american-style pork spareribs
1 cup (280g) crunchy peanut butter
½ cup (125ml) boiling water
⅓ cup (115g) honey
2 tablespoons sweet chilli sauce
2 tablespoons dark soy sauce
2 cloves garlic, crushed
1 fresh small red thai chilli, chopped finely
1 tablespoon lime juice
coleslaw
3 cups (240g) finely shredded savoy cabbage
3 cups (240g) finely shredded red cabbage
2 medium carrots (240g), grated finely
4 green onions, sliced thinly
1 cup loosely packed fresh flat-leaf parsley leaves
⅓ cup (100g) mayonnaise
¼ cup (60g) sour cream
2 tablespoons white wine vinegar

1 Preheat oven to 180°C/160°C fan-forced.
2 Combine ribs with remaining ingredients in shallow large baking dish; roast, covered, 40 minutes.
3 Meanwhile, make coleslaw.
4 Preheat grill.
5 Grill ribs, turning and basting occasionally with juices, about 20 minutes or until browned.
6 Cut ribs into serving-sized pieces; serve with coleslaw.
coleslaw Combine ingredients in large bowl. Refrigerate, covered, until required.
nutritional count per serving 38.5g total fat (10g saturated fat); 2667kJ (638 cal); 22.1g carbohydrate; 47.6g protein; 7.7g fibre

The eggplant can be brushed with 1 tablespoon
olive oil and cooked under the grill, if you prefer.
Beef mince can be used in place of the lamb mince.
Serve with the Greek Salad on page 9, if you like.

MOUSSAKA PARCELS

preparation time 40 minutes (plus standing time) | cooking time 40 minutes | serves 6

1 Cut each eggplant lengthways into 10 slices; discard edge pieces.
2 Cook eggplant, in batches, in heated oiled large frying pan; drain on absorbent paper.
3 Heat oil in same pan; cook onion and garlic, stirring, until onion softens. Add mince and spices; cook, stirring, until browned. Add paste, wine and half the sauce; bring to the boil. Reduce heat; simmer, covered, 30 minutes. Uncover; simmer about 10 minutes or until sauce thickens slightly. Remove from heat; stir in parsley.
4 Meanwhile, make cheese sauce.
5 Preheat oven to 200°C/180°C fan-forced.
6 Lay two slices of eggplant, slightly overlapping on board; spread ⅓ cup lamb mixture across centre of eggplant. Roll eggplant tightly to enclose filling; place seam-side down in shallow 2-litre (8-cup) ovenproof dish. Repeat with remaining eggplant and lamb mixture.
7 Pour remaining tomato pasta sauce over eggplant parcels; top with cheese sauce, sprinkle with cheese and extra cinnamon. Bake, uncovered, 20 minutes or until browned lightly.
cheese sauce Melt butter in medium saucepan; stir in flour. Cook, stirring, until mixture bubbles and thickens. Gradually stir in milk; cook, stirring, until sauce boils and thickens. Remove from heat; stir in cheese, then egg.
nutritional count per serving 28.6g total fat (13.5g saturated fat); 2437kJ (583 cal); 27.7g carbohydrate; 45.8g protein; 9.3g fibre

3 large eggplants (1.5kg)
1 tablespoon olive oil
1 medium brown onion (150g), chopped finely
2 cloves garlic, crushed
1kg lamb mince
1 teaspoon ground cinnamon
¼ teaspoon ground nutmeg
¼ cup (70g) tomato paste
½ cup (125ml) dry red wine
700g bottled tomato pasta sauce
½ cup finely chopped fresh flat-leaf parsley
¼ cup (20g) finely grated parmesan cheese
pinch ground cinnamon, extra
cheese sauce
50g melted butter
¼ cup (35g) plain flour
1½ cups (375ml) hot milk
¼ cup (20g) finely grated parmesan cheese
1 egg, beaten lightly

49

The best thing about cooking lamb shanks is they require very little attention, but taste oh-so-good. You can halve the recipe to serve four.

TOMATO BRAISED LAMB SHANKS WITH CREAMY POLENTA

preparation time 30 minutes | cooking time 3 hours 30 minutes | serves 8

2 tablespoons olive oil
16 french-trimmed lamb shanks
    (4kg)
1 large red onion (300g),
    sliced thinly
1 clove garlic, crushed
2 tablespoons tomato paste
1 cup (250ml) dry red wine
2 cups (500ml) chicken stock
1 cup (250ml) water
400g can diced tomatoes
2 tablespoons coarsely chopped
    fresh rosemary
creamy polenta
3 cups (750ml) water
2 cups (500ml) milk
1 cup (250ml) chicken stock
1½ cups (250g) polenta
½ cup (40g) coarsely grated
    parmesan cheese
1 cup (250ml) cream

1 Preheat oven to 200°C/180°C fan-forced.
2 Heat half the oil in large baking dish; brown lamb, in batches.
3 Heat remaining oil in same dish; cook onion and garlic, stirring, until onion softens. Add paste; cook, stirring, 2 minutes. Add wine; bring to the boil. Boil, uncovered, until liquid reduces by about half.
4 Return lamb to dish with stock, the water, undrained tomatoes and rosemary; cover, cook in oven, turning lamb occasionally, about 3 hours.
5 Remove lamb from dish; cover to keep warm. Reserve pan juices.
6 Meanwhile, make creamy polenta.
7 Divide polenta among serving plates; top with lamb, drizzle with juices.
creamy polenta Bring the water, milk and stock to the boil in medium saucepan; gradually stir in polenta. Cook, stirring, about 5 minutes or until polenta thickens slightly. Stir in cheese and cream.
nutritional count per serving 28g total fat (14.8g saturated fat); 2826kJ (676 cal); 30.3g carbohydrate; 69.1g protein; 2.3g fibre

The apple raspberry sauce can be made a day ahead; store, covered, in the refrigerator.

ROAST PORK WITH APPLE RASPBERRY SAUCE

preparation time 30 minutes (plus standing time) | cooking time 1 hour 30 minutes | serves 6

1 Make apple raspberry sauce.

2 Preheat oven to 240°C/220°C fan-forced.

3 Using sharp knife, score pork by making shallow cuts diagonally in both directions at 1cm intervals. Rub pork all over with oil; rub salt all over rind. Place pork, rind-side up, on oiled wire rack over large shallow baking dish; roast 30 minutes. Reduce temperature to 180°C/160°C fan-forced; roast pork about 1 hour. Cover pork loosely with foil; stand 20 minutes.

4 Meanwhile, boil, steam or microwave potatoes until tender; drain.

5 Melt butter in large frying pan; cook onion and garlic, stirring, until onion softens. Add cabbage and vinegar; cook, stirring, until cabbage is tender. Add potatoes; cook, stirring, until combined.

6 Serve pork with cabbage and apple raspberry sauce.

apple raspberry sauce Peel, core and quarter apples; slice thinly. Melt butter in medium saucepan; cook apple, stirring, about 5 minutes or until browned lightly. Add sugar, the water and berries; cook, stirring, 5 minutes or until berries soften and sauce thickens slightly.

nutritional count per serving 42.1g total fat (17.5g saturated fat); 2955kJ (707 cal); 45.8g carbohydrate; 32.3g protein; 9.5g fibre

1 x 6 cutlet pork rack (1.4kg),
  rind on
1 tablespoon olive oil
1 tablespoon sea salt flakes
1kg kipfler potatoes,
  chopped coarsely
50g butter
1 medium red onion (170g),
  sliced thinly
1 clove garlic, crushed
6 cups (480g) finely shredded
  cabbage
¼ cup (60ml) cider vinegar
apple raspberry sauce
4 medium apples (600g)
40g butter
¼ cup (55g) caster sugar
½ cup (125ml) water
1 cup (150g) fresh or frozen
  raspberries

TRADITIONAL TURKEY WITH CORN BREAD AND CANDIED SWEET POTATO PIE

preparation time 1 hour (plus standing time) | cooking time 3 hours 30 minutes | serves 8

4kg turkey
1 cup (250ml) water
40g butter, melted
⅓ cup (50g) plain flour
1 cup (250ml) dry white wine
1 litre (4 cups) chicken stock
corn bread
½ cup (75g) self-raising flour
½ cup (85g) cornmeal
¼ cup (30g) coarsely grated
    cheddar cheese
125g can creamed corn
125g can corn kernels,
    rinsed, drained
⅓ cup (80ml) buttermilk
1 egg, beaten lightly
30g butter, melted
forcemeat stuffing
40g butter
1 large brown onion (200g),
    chopped finely
4 thin slices prosciutto (60g),
    chopped finely
500g chicken mince
1 cup (70g) stale breadcrumbs
½ cup (60g) coarsely chopped
    roasted pecans
⅓ cup finely chopped fresh
    flat-leaf parsley
2 tablespoons finely chopped
    fresh sage
candied sweet potato pie
2 large kumara (1kg),
    chopped coarsely
80g butter
2 eggs, beaten lightly
⅓ cup (50g) plain flour
⅓ cup (75g) firmly packed
    brown sugar
½ teaspoon ground cinnamon
¼ teaspoon ground ginger
¾ cup (90g) coarsely chopped
    roasted pecans

1 Make corn bread.
2 Make forcemeat stuffing.
3 Reduce oven temperature to 180°C/160°C fan-forced.
4 Fill neck cavity of turkey with some of the stuffing; secure skin with toothpicks or small skewers to enclose stuffing. Fill large cavity with remaining stuffing; secure skin. Tie legs together with kitchen string.
5 Place turkey on oiled wire rack in shallow large baking dish; pour the water into dish. Brush turkey all over with butter. Roast, covered, 2 hours. Uncover turkey; roast about 1 hour, basting occasionally with dish juices, until turkey is cooked through.
6 Meanwhile, make candied sweet potato pie.
7 Remove turkey from dish; reserve ⅓ cup juices from dish. Cover turkey; stand 20 minutes.
8 Heat reserved juices in same dish. Add flour; cook, stirring, until mixture is well browned. Gradually stir in wine and stock; stir until gravy boils and thickens. Strain gravy into heatproof jug.
9 Serve turkey with gravy, corn bread and candied sweet potato pie.
corn bread Preheat oven to 200°C/180°C fan-forced. Grease 8cm x 26cm bar cake pan; line base with baking paper, extending paper 5cm over long sides. Sift flour into medium bowl; stir in cornmeal and cheese. Stir in combined remaining ingredients. Spread mixture into pan; bake, about 30 minutes. Stand 10 minutes; turn onto wire rack to cool.
forcemeat stuffing Melt butter in medium frying pan; cook onion and prosciutto, stirring, until onion softens. Combine onion mixture in medium bowl with remaining ingredients.
candied sweet potato pie Boil, steam or microwave kumara until tender; drain. Mash kumara in medium bowl with half of the butter until smooth; stir in egg. Spread mixture into oiled 2-litre (8-cup) ovenproof dish. Combine flour, sugar and spices in small bowl; using fingertips, rub in remaining butter. Stir in nuts. Sprinkle nut mixture over kumara; bake, uncovered, about 30 minutes or until browned.
nutritional count per serving 75.2g total fat (26.7g saturated fat); 5338kJ (1277 cal); 61.8g carbohydrate; 81.2g protein; 6.3g fibre

Corn bread can be made a day
ahead; store in an airtight container.

The chilli paste made in this recipe also tastes great rubbed over a whole chicken or fish before being roasted.

SPICY BARBECUED SPATCHCOCK WITH BAKED RÖSTI AND SWEET CAPSICUM PUREE

preparation time 40 minutes (plus refrigeration time) | cooking time 1 hour | serves 8

1 Using scissors, cut along both sides of spatchcocks' backbones, discard backbones. Halve each spatchcock along breastbone. Using small sharp knife pierce spatchcocks all over.

2 Blend or process oil, chilli, mustard, rind, juice and garlic until smooth. Reserve ½ cup chilli mixture; combine remaining chilli mixture and spatchcock in large bowl. Cover; refrigerate 3 hours or overnight.

3 Cook spatchcock on heated oiled grill plate (or grill or barbecue), covered, 30 minutes. Uncover spatchcock; cook about 30 minutes.

4 Meanwhile, preheat oven to 200°C/180°C fan-forced. Grease sixteen ⅓-cup (80ml) muffin pan holes.

5 To make rösti, coarsely grate potatoes into large bowl; stir in salt. Squeeze out excess liquid; stir in butter. Divide mixture among 16 of the pan holes, pressing mixture down firmly. Bake 30 minutes or until browned and crisp.

6 Halve capsicum; discard seeds and membranes. Place on oven tray; grill or roast, skin-side up, until skin blisters and blackens. Cover capsicum pieces with plastic or paper for 5 minutes; peel away skin. Blend or process capsicum with reserved chilli mixture until smooth.

7 Serve spatchcock with rösti, sweet capsicum puree and spinach leaves.

nutritional count per serving 54.8g total fat (14.2g saturated fat); 2926kJ (700 cal); 21.3g carbohydrate; 29.8g protein; 4.3g fibre

4 x 500g spatchcocks
1 cup (250ml) olive oil
3 fresh small red thai chillies, chopped coarsely
2 tablespoons dijon mustard
1 tablespoon finely grated lemon rind
⅓ cup (80ml) lemon juice
2 cloves garlic, quartered
5 medium potatoes (1kg)
1 teaspoon course cooking salt
60g butter, melted
3 large red capsicums (1kg)
80g baby spinach leaves

If you're not mad about marinara mix, you can use the same weight of prawns in the risotto instead – just shell and devein the prawns, leaving the tails intact and add to the recipe when you would've added the marinara mix. Preserved lemon tastes great in risotto, too – if you have some at home, use it in place of the lemon rind. Finely chop about 1 teaspoon of trimmed and well-rinsed preserved lemon rind, then stir into the risotto before serving.

SEAFOOD RISOTTO

preparation time 35 minutes | cooking time 40 minutes | serves 8

1.5 litres (6 cups) chicken stock
2 cups (500ml) water
2 tablespoons olive oil
1 medium leek (350g), sliced thinly
1 fresh small red thai chilli, chopped finely
3 cups (600g) arborio rice
pinch saffron threads
1 cup (250ml) dry white wine
2 tablespoons tomato paste
1.5kg marinara mix
1 cup (120g) frozen peas
2 teaspoons finely grated lemon rind
1 cup loosely packed fresh flat-leaf parsley leaves

1 Combine stock and the water in medium saucepan; bring to the boil. Simmer, covered.
2 Heat oil in large saucepan; cook leek and chilli, stirring, until leek softens. Add rice and saffron; stir to coat in leek mixture. Add wine and paste; cook, stirring, until wine has almost evaporated.
3 Add ½ cup simmering stock to the rice mixture. Cook, stirring, over low heat, until liquid is absorbed. Continue adding stock mixture, in ½ cup batches, stirring until liquid is absorbed after each addition. Total cooking time should be about 30 minutes.
4 Add marinara mix and peas; mix gently. Simmer, covered, 5 minutes. Uncover; simmer until all stock has been absorbed and seafood is tender.
5 Stir in rind and parsley.
nutritional count per serving 5.9g total fat (1.1g saturated fat); 1547kJ (370 cal); 63.2g carbohydrate; 8.9g protein; 2.9g fibre

Vindaloo hails from the former Portuguese colony of Goa. Portuguese for vinegar and garlic, vindaloo is a highly flavoured, but also fiercely hot curry. If you like, you can reduce the amount of chilli in the recipe. Vindaloo is great topped with fresh coriander leaves and served with steamed rice.

PORK AND VEGETABLE VINDALOO

preparation time 30 minutes | cooking time 1 hour | serves 6

1 Dry-fry spices in small frying pan, stirring, until fragrant; cool.
2 Blend or process spices, garlic, chilli, ginger, onion and vinegar until mixture forms a smooth paste.
3 Heat half the oil in large saucepan; cook pork, in batches, until browned.
4 Heat remaining oil in same pan; cook paste, stirring, 5 minutes. Return pork to pan with stock; bring to the boil. Reduce heat; simmer, covered, 30 minutes. Add potato, carrot and beans; simmer, uncovered, about 30 minutes or until pork is tender and sauce thickens slightly.
nutritional count per serving 19.9g total fat (5.4g saturated fat); 1664kJ (398 cal); 13.6g carbohydrate; 39.3g protein; 3.8g fibre

2 teaspoons cumin seeds
2 teaspoons garam masala
1 teaspoon ground cinnamon
2 cloves garlic, quartered
4 fresh small red thai chillies, chopped coarsely
2cm piece fresh ginger (10g), sliced thinly
1 large brown onion (200g) chopped coarsely
2 tablespoons white vinegar
2 tablespoons vegetable oil
1kg boneless pork shoulder, cut into 2cm pieces
2 cups (500ml) beef stock
2 medium potatoes (400g), cut into 2cm pieces
2 medium carrots (240g), cut into 2cm pieces
150g green beans, trimmed, chopped coarsely

We used snapper in this recipe, but a fish like salmon would work well, too – it may need slightly less cooking time, depending on how you like your salmon cooked.

BARBECUED FISH WITH VEGETABLE PARCELS

preparation time 20 minutes | cooking time 40 minutes | serves 8

1 whole fish (2kg)
1 clove garlic, sliced thinly
3 sprigs fresh rosemary,
   cut into 3cm lengths
1 medium lemon (140g),
   sliced thinly
40g butter
2 large zucchinis (300g)
2 trimmed corn cobs (500g),
   sliced thickly
2 medium red capsicums (400g),
   sliced thickly
1 large red onion (300g),
   cut into wedges
lemon herb butter
160g butter, softened
1 clove garlic, crushed
2 teaspoons finely grated
   lemon rind
2 teaspoons finely chopped
   fresh rosemary

1 Make lemon herb butter.
2 Meanwhile, place fish on board; score fish both sides through thickest part of flesh. Push garlic and rosemary into cuts; fill cavity with a third of the lemon slices.
3 Place a long piece of baking paper on bench; place half of the remaining lemon slices on paper. Place fish on lemon; top with remaining lemon then butter. Fold paper over fish to completely enclose, then wrap tightly in foil.
4 Cook fish on heated oiled grill plate (or grill or barbecue) 20 minutes; turn, cook about 20 minutes.
5 Meanwhile, cut zucchini in half crossways; cut each half lengthways into six. Combine zucchini with remaining ingredients in large bowl. Place eight 30cm foil squares on bench; divide vegetable mixture among foil squares. Gather corners of squares together; fold to enclose vegetables securely.
6 Cook parcels on heated oiled flat plate until vegetables are tender.
7 Open vegetable parcels; top with slices of lemon herb butter. Serve with fish.
lemon herb butter Combine ingredients in small bowl. Place on piece of plastic wrap; shape into 6cm log, wrap tightly. Freeze until firm; cut into eight slices.
nutritional count per serving 24.2g total fat (14.5g saturated fat); 1664kJ (398 cal); 12.4g carbohydrate; 30.9g protein; 4.2g fibre

Serve the gnocchi topped with crispy prosciutto – just grill the
prosciutto until it begins to crisp and curl up on the sides.
It's important to drain the potatoes well, to ensure you have light,
fluffy gnocchi; if the dough is too wet, the gnocchi will be stodgy.
If you do not have a ricer or mouli, simply use the back of a large
spoon to push the potatoes through a fine sieve into a large bowl.

GNOCCHI WITH ROASTED KUMARA, SPINACH AND PINE NUTS

preparation time 1 hour (plus refrigeration time) | cooking time 30 minutes | serves 6

1 Boil, steam or microwave whole, unpeeled potatoes until tender; drain. Cool potatoes for 10 minutes; peel. Mash potatoes through ricer or mouli into large bowl; stir in milk and garlic. Stir in egg yolks, grated cheese and flour.

2 Roll one-quarter of dough on floured board into 2cm-thick sausage; cut into 2cm lengths. Press each piece of dough against back of fork. Place gnocchi on floured tray. Repeat with remaining dough. Cover gnocchi; refrigerate 1 hour.

3 Preheat oven to 200°C/180°C fan-forced.

4 Combine kumara and half the oil in shallow medium baking dish; roast about 30 minutes or until tender.

5 Meanwhile, cook gnocchi, in batches, in large saucepan of boiling water until gnocchi float to surface; drain.

6 Melt butter in medium frying pan with the remaining oil; cook tomato and sage, stirring, 2 minutes or until tomato softens slightly and butter is browned lightly.

7 Combine gnocchi, kumara, tomato mixture and remaining ingredients in large bowl. You can serve gnocchi sprinkled with extra flaked parmesan.

nutritional count per serving 45.5g total fat (21.8g saturated fat); 3302kJ (790 cal); 74.5g carbohydrate; 18g protein; 8.5g fibre

1.5 kg potatoes
¼ cup (60ml) milk
1 clove garlic, crushed
3 egg yolks
½ cup (40g) finely grated
    parmesan cheese
1½ cups (225g) plain flour
2 medium kumara (800g),
    cut into 1cm pieces
2 tablespoons olive oil
200g unsalted butter, chopped
3 medium tomatoes (450g),
    chopped finely
¾ cup loosely packed fresh
    sage leaves
60g baby spinach leaves
½ cup (40g) flaked parmesan cheese
⅓ cup (50g) roasted pine nuts

This recipe freezes well; you could double the recipe and freeze one batch for a rainy day. Serve with a baby spinach, grape tomato and celery salad for a delicious family dinner.

MACARONI CHEESE WITH OLIVES

preparation time 10 minutes | cooking time 25 minutes | serves 4

375g elbow macaroni
60g butter
1 small red onion (100g), sliced thinly
1 clove garlic, crushed
1 medium red capsicum (200g), sliced thinly
150g mushrooms, sliced thinly
⅓ cup (50g) plain flour
3 cups (750ml) milk
⅓ cup (95g) tomato paste
⅓ cup (40g) seeded black olives, halved
½ cup finely chopped fresh basil
1½ cups (150g) coarsely grated pizza cheese

1 Cook pasta in large saucepan of boiling water until just tender; drain.
2 Meanwhile, melt butter in large saucepan; cook onion, garlic, capsicum and mushrooms, stirring, until vegetables soften. Add flour; cook, stirring, until mixture bubbles and thickens. Gradually stir in milk. Add paste; cook, stirring, until sauce boils and thickens.
3 Preheat grill.
4 Stir pasta, olives, basil and half the cheese into sauce. Place mixture in deep 2-litre (8-cup) ovenproof dish; sprinkle with remaining cheese. Grill until cheese melts and is browned lightly.
nutritional count per serving 29.5g total fat (18.4g saturated fat); 3223kJ (771 cal); 90.1g carbohydrate; 32.4g protein; 6.7g fibre

FAMILY DINNERS

FETTUCCINE BOLOGNESE

preparation time 20 minutes | cooking time 40 minutes | serves 4

1 tablespoon olive oil
1 large brown onion (200g),
 chopped finely
2 cloves garlic, crushed
600g beef mince
¼ cup (70g) tomato paste
1 cup (125ml) beef stock
2 x 400g cans diced tomatoes
⅓ cup finely chopped fresh
 flat-leaf parsley
1 tablespoon finely chopped
 fresh oregano
375g fettuccine
½ cup flaked parmesan cheese

1 Heat oil in large frying pan; cook onion and garlic, stirring, until onion softens.
2 Add mince; cook, stirring, until browned. Add paste, stock and undrained tomatoes; bring to the boil. Reduce heat; simmer, covered, 20 minutes. Uncover; simmer about 10 minutes or until thickened slightly. Remove from heat; stir in herbs.
3 Meanwhile, cook pasta in large saucepan of boiling water until tender; drain.
4 Serve fettuccine topped with bolognese and cheese.
nutritional count per serving 20g total fat (7.4g saturated fat); 2893kJ (692 cal); 75g carbohydrate; 48.4g protein; 7.3g fibre

VARIATIONS
chilli con carne Add 1 teaspoon ground cumin and 1 teaspoon dried chilli flakes with mince at step 2. Add rinsed and drained 420g can four-bean mix at end of step 2. Omit steps 3 and 4. Serve with 3 cups steamed rice instead of the pasta.
nutritional count per serving 16g total fat (5.1g saturated fat); 2399kJ (574 cal); 60.5g carbohydrate; 41.4g protein; 9.5g fibre

cottage pie Add 2 cups frozen pea, corn and carrot mixture for last 5 minutes of step 2 cooking time. Omit steps 3 and 4. Boil, steam or microwave 800g coarsely chopped potatoes until tender; drain. Mash in medium bowl with 20g butter and ½ cup hot milk until smooth. Place mince mixture in deep 2-litre (8-cup) ovenproof dish; top with potato, sprinkle with ½ cup coarsely grated cheddar cheese. Grill 10 minutes or until browned lightly.
nutritional count per serving 26.4g total fat (11.7g saturated fat); 2558kJ (612 cal); 42.1g carbohydrate; 46.3g protein; 10.4g fibre

We used fettuccine in this recipe, but
you can use the pasta of your choice.
The bolognese sauce can be frozen in an
airtight container for up to three months.

Broccolini is a cross between broccoli and chinese kale; it resembles broccoli in appearance, but is milder and sweeter in taste. It has long asparagus-like stems and a long loose floret, both completely edible. Baby buk choy or gai lan work well in this stir-fry, too; use in place of the broccolini.

MONGOLIAN LAMB AND NOODLE STIR-FRY

preparation time 20 minutes | cooking time 20 minutes | serves 4

600g lamb backstrap, sliced thinly
⅓ cup (80ml) sweet sherry
2 tablespoons dark soy sauce
2 tablespoons sweet chilli sauce
2 tablespoons peanut oil
1 large brown onion (200g),
    sliced thinly
2 cloves garlic, crushed
1 medium green capsicum (200g),
    sliced thinly
175g broccolini,
    cut into 3cm lengths
1 tablespoon brown sugar
1 teaspoon sesame oil
⅓ cup (80ml) chicken stock
400g hokkien noodles

1 Combine lamb with half the sherry, half the soy sauce and half the sweet chilli sauce in medium bowl.
2 Heat half the peanut oil in wok; stir-fry lamb, in batches, until browned.
3 Heat remaining peanut oil in wok; stir-fry onion and garlic until onion softens. Add capsicum and broccolini; stir-fry until vegetables are tender.
4 Return lamb to wok with remaining ingredients; stir-fry until hot.
nutritional count per serving 17.4g total fat (4.5g saturated fat); 2600kJ (622 cal); 63.6g carbohydrate; 44.5g protein; 5.4g fibre

Garlic prawns can be served with steamed rice or pasta.

GARLIC PRAWNS

preparation time 15 minutes | cooking time 15 minutes | serves 4

1 Shell and devein prawns, leaving tails intact. Combine prawns, garlic and chilli in medium bowl.
2 Heat half the oil in large frying pan; cook prawns, stirring, until changed in colour. Remove from pan.
3 Heat remaining oil in same pan; cook capsicums, stirring, until tender. Return prawns to pan with stock, cream and juice; bring to the boil. Reduce heat; simmer, uncovered, about 5 minutes or until sauce thickens slightly. Remove from heat; stir in parsley.
nutritional count per serving 42.6g total fat (22.9g saturated fat); 2169kJ (519 cal); 5.4g carbohydrate; 28.9g protein; 1.4g fibre

1kg uncooked medium king
   prawns
4 cloves garlic, crushed
2 fresh small red thai chillies,
   chopped finely
2 tablespoons olive oil
1 medium red capsicum (200g),
   sliced thinly
1 medium green capsicum (200g),
   sliced thinly
½ cup (125ml) chicken stock
300ml cream
1 tablespoon lemon juice
1 tablespoon finely chopped fresh
   flat-leaf parsley

BACON-WRAPPED STEAKS WITH TARRAGON BUTTER

preparation time 10 minutes (plus freezing and standing time) | cooking time 20 minutes | serves 4

60g butter, softened
1 clove garlic, crushed
2 teaspoons finely chopped
   fresh tarragon
2 teaspoons finely grated
   lemon rind
3 medium potatoes (600g)
4 rindless bacon rashers (260g)
4 x 150g beef fillet steaks

1 Combine butter, garlic, tarragon and rind in small bowl. Place on piece of plastic wrap; shape into 6cm log, wrap tightly. Freeze until firm.
2 Boil, steam or microwave potatoes until tender; drain. Cool slightly; slice thickly.
3 Meanwhile, wrap bacon around beef; secure with toothpicks. Cook in heated oiled large frying pan until cooked as desired. Cover beef; stand 5 minutes.
4 Meanwhile, add potato to same pan, cook until brown.
5 Remove butter from freezer; cut into four slices.
6 Place potato on serving plates; top with beef, then butter slices.
nutritional count per serving 25g total fat (13.2g saturated fat); 2061kJ (493 cal); 17.2g carbohydrate; 48.7g protein; 2.2g fibre

Often called the king of herbs by the French, tarragon is used as the essential flavouring for many of their classic sauces, like béarnaise and tartare. It is available from most supermarkets, however, if you can't find it, use the same quantity of any fresh herb you like — basil tastes particularly good with this recipe. Serve the steak with a simple rocket, pear and parmesan salad.

SWEET AND SOUR PORK

preparation time 20 minutes | cooking time 20 minutes | serves 4

1 Combine pork with sherry and 2 tablespoons of the soy sauce in medium bowl; coat pork in flour, shake off excess.
2 Heat oil in wok; deep-fry pork, in batches, until browned and crisp. Drain on absorbent paper. (Strain oil, save for another use.)
3 Heat extra oil in wok; stir-fry onion and garlic until onion softens. Add capsicums and carrot; stir-fry until vegetables are tender. Return pork to wok with pineapple, peas, remaining soy sauce, stock, tomato sauce, vinegar and sugar; stir-fry until hot. Remove from heat; stir in coriander.
nutritional count per serving 20.2g total fat (3.6g saturated fat); 2717kJ (650 cal); 57.7g carbohydrate; 53.7g protein; 7.5g fibre

800g pork fillet, sliced thinly
1 tablespoon sweet sherry
½ cup (125ml) light soy sauce
¾ cup (110g) plain flour
vegetable oil, for deep-frying
1 tablespoon vegetable oil, extra
1 medium red onion (170g),
    chopped coarsely
2 cloves garlic, crushed
1 medium red capsicum (200g),
    chopped coarsely
1 medium green capsicum (200g),
    chopped coarsely
1 medium carrot (120g),
    sliced thinly
500g fresh pineapple,
    chopped coarsely
150g sugar snap peas, trimmed
⅓ cup (80ml) chicken stock
¼ cup (70g) tomato sauce
¼ cup (60ml) white vinegar
¼ cup (55g) white sugar
½ cup loosely packed fresh
    coriander leaves

You will need half a pineapple (900g) to get the amount of fresh pineapple required for this recipe. If you don't have any fresh pineapple, you can use a small can of drained pineapple, instead.
Steamed white rice is perfect with this dish.

Mashed potato goes great
with this recipe. Simply
boil, steam or microwave
1kg coarsely chopped potato
until tender, then drain. Mash
the potato in a large bowl
until smooth with ⅔ cup
warmed buttermilk or cream.

ROSEMARY LAMB SKEWERS

preparation time 15 minutes | cooking time 20 minutes | serves 4

8 sprigs fresh rosemary
600g lamb mince
1 egg yolk
2 cloves garlic, crushed
1 tablespoon tomato paste
⅓ cup (25g) stale breadcrumbs
¼ cup (60ml) olive oil
1 large brown onion (200g),
   sliced thinly
1 tablespoon plain flour
1 cup (250ml) beef stock
2 medium tomatoes (300g),
   chopped coarsely

1 Remove two-thirds of the leaves from the bottom part of each rosemary sprig to make skewers. Finely chop 2 teaspoons of the leaves and reserve.
2 Combine mince, egg yolk, garlic, paste, breadcrumbs and reserved rosemary in medium bowl. Shape lamb mixture into sausage shapes on rosemary skewers.
3 Heat 1 tablespoon of the oil in large frying pan; cook skewers until browned and cooked through. Cover to keep warm.
4 Heat remaining oil in same pan; cook onion, stirring, until soft. Add flour; cook, stirring, until mixture bubbles and thickens. Gradually stir in stock until smooth. Add tomato; cook, stirring, until gravy boils and thickens.
5 Serve rosemary lamb skewers with gravy.
nutritional count per serving 26g total fat (7.1g saturated fat); 1781kJ (426 cal); 11.9g carbohydrate; 35.1g protein; 2.5g fibre

If blood oranges are in season, you can use them in place of regular oranges – they have a gorgeous salmon-coloured pulp and a slightly sweeter flavour than regular oranges.

CRUMBED LAMB CUTLETS WITH ORANGE, COUSCOUS AND SPINACH SALAD

preparation time 20 minutes | cooking time 20 minutes | serves 4

1 Combine breadcrumbs and spices in small shallow bowl.
2 Coat lamb in flour; shake off excess. Dip in egg, then in crumb mixture to coat.
3 Heat oil in large frying pan; shallow-fry lamb, in batches, until cooked as desired. Drain on absorbent paper.
4 Meanwhile, combine couscous with the water in large heatproof bowl, cover; stand about 5 minutes or until water is absorbed, fluffing with fork occasionally.
5 Segment oranges over small bowl; reserve ¼ cup juice.
6 Add orange segments, reserved juice and remaining ingredients to couscous; mix well.
7 Serve cutlets with orange, couscous and spinach salad.
nutritional count per serving 60.1g total fat (18.6g saturated fat); 3658kJ (875 cal); 49.1g carbohydrate; 33.6g protein; 4.2g fibre

⅔ cup (50g) stale breadcrumbs
2 teaspoons sweet paprika
2 teaspoons ground cumin
½ teaspoon ground cardamom
12 french-trimmed lamb cutlets (600g)
¼ cup (35g) plain flour
1 egg, beaten lightly
vegetable oil, for shallow-frying
½ cup (100g) couscous
½ cup (125ml) boiling water
2 medium oranges (480g)
1 cup (120g) seeded black olives
200g fetta cheese, cut into 1cm pieces
100g baby spinach leaves
1 small red onion (100g), sliced thinly
⅓ cup (80ml) olive oil
2 tablespoons white wine vinegar

SPAGHETTI AND MEATBALLS

preparation time 25 minutes | cooking time 25 minutes | serves 4

500g pork and veal mince
½ cup (35g) stale breadcrumbs
1 egg
¼ cup (20g) finely grated
    parmesan cheese
1 tablespoon olive oil
1 medium brown onion (150g),
    chopped coarsely
2 cloves garlic, quartered
1 fresh small red thai chilli
6 anchovy fillets
1 cup (150g) drained sun-dried
    tomatoes
¼ cup (70g) tomato paste
1 cup (250ml) chicken stock
12 pimiento-stuffed olives,
    sliced thinly
375g spaghetti
⅓ cup coarsely chopped fresh
    flat-leaf parsley

1 Combine mince, breadcrumbs, egg and cheese in medium bowl; roll level tablespoons of mixture into balls.
2 Heat oil in medium frying pan; cook meatballs, uncovered, until browned.
3 Blend or process onion, garlic, chilli, anchovy, tomatoes and paste until smooth. Combine tomato mixture with stock in medium saucepan; bring to the boil. Add meatballs and olives; simmer, uncovered, 15 minutes.
4 Meanwhile, cook spaghetti in large saucepan of boiling water until tender; drain.
5 Serve spaghetti topped with meatballs and sauce; sprinkle with parsley.
nutritional count per serving 20.6g total fat (6.3g saturated fat); 2964kJ (709 cal); 78.8g carbohydrate; 47.5g protein; 7.9g fibre

Anchovies are always a feature in this popular Italian pasta, however, if you're cooking for someone who doesn't like them, you can omit them. A teaspoon of baby capers can be added to the tomato mixture for an extra-salty sensation.

Parsnip is a large, white root vegetable, not dissimilar in flavour to carrot. If you prefer, you can substitute the same amount of kumara for the parsnip in the mash.

CARAMELISED ONION AND PROSCIUTTO GLAZED MEATLOAF

preparation time 40 minutes | cooking time 1 hour 30 minutes | serves 4

1 Heat oil in large frying pan; cook onion, stirring, about 5 minutes or until soft and browned lightly. Add sugar and vinegar; cook, stirring, about 15 minutes or until onion is caramelised. Cool.

2 Meanwhile, preheat oven to 200°C/180°C fan-forced. Grease 14cm x 21cm loaf pan; line base and long sides of pan with prosciutto slices, allowing 7cm overhang on long sides of pan.

3 Combine mince, egg, breadcrumbs, paste and garlic in large bowl. Press two-thirds of the beef mixture into pan; top with onion mixture, cover with remaining beef mixture. Fold prosciutto slices over to cover beef mixture.

4 Bake, covered, 40 minutes. Remove loaf from oven. Drain excess juices from pan.

5 Turn pan upside-down onto foil-lined oven tray; remove pan. Combine half the sauces, half the mustard and half the extra sugar in small bowl. Brush loaf with sauce mixture; bake, uncovered, basting occasionally with sauce mixture, about 20 minutes or until loaf is cooked through. Stand 10 minutes; slice thickly.

6 Meanwhile, make parsnip mash.

7 To make mustard glaze, combine the water with remaining sauces, mustard and sugar in small saucepan; stir over low heat until sugar dissolves. Bring to the boil; reduce heat. Simmer, uncovered, 2 minutes.

8 Serve meatloaf with parsnip mash and mustard glaze.

parsnip mash Boil, steam or microwave potato and parsnip until tender; drain. Mash vegetables in large bowl with butter and milk until smooth.

nutritional count per serving 36.5g total fat (15.6g saturated fat); 4000kJ (957 cal); 81.1g carbohydrate; 71.3g protein; 8g fibre

1 tablespoon olive oil
2 large brown onions (400g), sliced thinly
¼ cup (55g) firmly packed brown sugar
¼ cup (60ml) cider vinegar
12 slices prosciutto (180g)
1kg beef mince
1 egg
1 cup (70g) stale breadcrumbs
2 tablespoons tomato paste
1 clove garlic, crushed
⅓ cup (95g) tomato sauce
⅓ cup (95g) barbecue sauce
2 tablespoons wholegrain mustard
2 tablespoons brown sugar, extra
¼ cup (60ml) water

parsnip mash
3 medium potatoes (600g), chopped coarsely
2 medium parsnips (500g), chopped coarsely
40g butter, chopped coarsely
½ cup (125ml) hot milk

Garam masala literally means "blended spices" in its northern Indian place of origin; it is based on varying proportions of cardamom, cinnamon, clove, coriander, fennel and cumin, roasted and ground together. Black pepper and chilli can be added for a hotter version. Steamed rice is a great accompaniment for this meal.

BUTTER CHICKEN DRUMSTICKS

preparation time 20 minutes | cooking time 30 minutes | serves 4

1 cup (150g) roasted unsalted cashews
2 teaspoons garam masala
2 teaspoons ground coriander
1 teaspoon ground cinnamon
½ teaspoon chilli powder
¼ teaspoon ground cardamom
2 cloves garlic, quartered
3cm piece fresh ginger (15g), grated
⅓ cup (95g) tomato paste
2 tablespoons lemon juice
¾ cup (180ml) buttermilk
60g butter
12 chicken drumsticks (1.8kg)
1½ cups (375ml) chicken stock
½ cup loosely packed fresh coriander leaves

1 Preheat oven to 200°C/180°C fan-forced.
2 Process nuts, spices, garlic, ginger, paste, juice and ¼ cup of the buttermilk until smooth.
3 Melt half the butter in large baking dish; cook chicken, in batches, until browned.
4 Melt remaining butter in same dish; cook spice mixture, stirring, about 3 minutes or until fragrant. Stir in stock and remaining buttermilk; bring to the boil. Return chicken to dish.
5 Roast, covered, 10 minutes. Uncover; roast about 10 minutes or until chicken is cooked through.
6 Serve chicken sprinkled with coriander.
nutritional count per serving 63.6g total fat (21.7g saturated fat); 3637kJ (870 cal); 13.1g carbohydrate; 60.9g protein; 3.8g fibre

Porcini, also known as cèpes, are the richest-flavoured mushrooms. Though expensive, they are so strongly-flavoured only a small amount is required for any particular dish. They are available from specialty food stores and some supermarkets.

MIXED MUSHROOM FETTUCCINE BOSCAIOLA

preparation time 20 minutes (plus standing time) | cooking time 20 minutes | serves 4

1 Combine porcini mushrooms and the water in small heatproof bowl; cover, stand 15 minutes or until mushrooms are tender. Drain; reserve soaking liquid, chop mushrooms coarsely.
2 Cook pasta in large saucepan of boiling water until tender; drain.
3 Meanwhile, heat oil in large frying pan; cook pancetta until crisp. Add all mushrooms and garlic; cook, stirring, until mushrooms are browned lightly. Add wine; bring to the boil. Boil, uncovered, until liquid has almost evaporated. Add cream, juice and reserved soaking liquid; simmer, uncovered, until sauce reduces by half and thickens slightly. Stir in cheese and chives.
4 Combine pasta and sauce in large bowl. Serve bowls of pasta sprinkled with extra parmesan cheese.
nutritional count per serving 45.5g total fat (26.1g saturated fat); 3390kJ (811 cal); 66.9g carbohydrate; 28.9g protein; 5.3g fibre

10g dried porcini mushrooms
¼ cup (60ml) boiling water
375g fettuccine
1 tablespoon olive oil
200g pancetta, chopped coarsely
100g button mushrooms,
    sliced thinly
100g swiss brown mushrooms,
    sliced thinly
1 flat mushroom (80g),
    sliced thinly
2 cloves garlic, crushed
¼ cup (60ml) dry white wine
300ml cream
1 tablespoon lemon juice
½ cup (40g) finely grated
    parmesan cheese
2 tablespoons coarsely chopped
    fresh chives
2 tablespoons finely grated
    parmesan cheese, extra

SPINACH AND RICOTTA-STUFFED CHICKEN PARMIGIANA

preparation time 15 minutes | cooking time 20 minutes | serves 4

8 x 100g chicken schnitzels
40g baby spinach leaves
1⅓ cups (320g) ricotta cheese
¼ cup (35g) plain flour
2 eggs
2 tablespoons milk
1½ cups (105g) stale breadcrumbs
vegetable oil, for shallow-frying
1 cup (260g) bottled
   tomato pasta sauce
1 cup (100g) coarsely grated
   mozzarella cheese

1 Preheat oven to 200°C/180°C fan-forced.
2 Top each schnitzel with spinach and cheese, leaving 1cm border around edges. Fold in half to secure filling; press down firmly.
3 Coat schnitzels in flour; shake off excess. Dip in combined egg and milk, then in breadcrumbs.
4 Heat oil in large frying pan; cook schnitzels, in batches, until browned and cooked through. Drain on absorbent paper.
5 Place schnitzels in oiled shallow large baking dish; top with sauce and cheese. Roast, uncovered, about 10 minutes or until cheese melts.
nutritional count per serving 40.2g total fat (15.3g saturated fat); 3194kJ (764 cal); 31.9g carbohydrate; 67.2g protein; 2.9g fibre

Secure schnitzels with toothpicks before coating and frying. Parmigiana goes well with homemade chips: simply cut 1kg unpeeled potatoes into 2cm-thick chips; boil, steam or microwave potatoes until just tender. Drain and completely dry with absorbent paper. Toss potato in a large bowl with a tablespoon of olive oil then place, in a single layer, on an oiled oven tray. Roast in a 240°C/220°C fan-forced oven about 25 minutes or until browned. We recommend russet burbank potatoes; they are good for both frying and baking.

Green curry is traditionally the hottest-flavoured Thai curry — if you find it too hot, however, you can always add a little extra coconut cream or chicken stock to reduce the heat. Serve with lime wedges.

GREEN CURRY WITH CHICKEN MEATBALLS

preparation time 30 minutes | cooking time 30 minutes | serves 4

1 Combine chicken, garlic, ginger and chopped coriander in large bowl; roll level tablespoons of mixture into balls.
2 Heat half the oil in large frying pan; cook chicken balls until browned.
3 Meanwhile, heat remaining oil in large saucepan; cook paste, stirring, about 2 minutes or until fragrant. Add coconut cream, sauce, juice and sugar; bring to the boil. Reduce heat; simmer, uncovered, 20 minutes. Add balls to pan with peas; simmer, uncovered, until balls are cooked through and peas are tender.
4 Serve bowls of curry sprinkled with sprouts, coriander leaves, nuts and chilli.

nutritional count per serving 80.5g total fat (44.7g saturated fat); 4243kJ (1015 cal); 19.7g carbohydrate; 50.6g protein; 9.1g fibre

800g chicken mince
2 cloves garlic, crushed
2cm piece fresh ginger (10g), grated
2 tablespoons finely chopped fresh coriander
2 tablespoons peanut oil
¼ cup (75g) green curry paste
2 x 400ml cans coconut cream
2 tablespoons fish sauce
2 tablespoons lime juice
1 tablespoon grated palm sugar
150g sugar snap peas, trimmed
1 cup (80g) bean sprouts
⅓ cup loosely packed fresh coriander leaves
⅔ cup (100g) roasted unsalted cashews
1 long green chilli, sliced thinly

This recipe is a great way to get kids to eat fish; it's cleverly disguised and tastes great, too. You can use roasted unsalted macadamias in place of the cashews, if you prefer.

CASHEW FISH FINGERS WITH MUSHY MINTED PEAS

preparation time 30 minutes (plus refrigeration time) | cooking time 15 minutes | serves 4

1kg firm white fish fillets, chopped coarsely
2 tablespoons coarsely chopped fresh flat-leaf parsley
2 teaspoons finely grated lemon rind
1 tablespoon lemon juice
1 clove garlic, quartered
½ cup (75g) plain flour
2 eggs, beaten lightly
⅔ cup (70g) packaged breadcrumbs
⅔ cup (90g) finely chopped roasted unsalted cashews
vegetable oil, for shallow-frying
2 cups (250g) frozen peas
20g butter
2 tablespoons finely chopped fresh mint

1 Grease 19cm x 29cm slice pan.
2 Process fish, parsley, rind, juice and garlic until smooth. Using spatula, press mixture evenly into pan; turn onto baking-paper-lined tray. Cut into eight x 19cm slices; cut each slice in half crossways to make 16 fingers. Cover; refrigerate 30 minutes.
3 Pat fish fingers with flour; shake off excess. Dip in egg, then in combined breadcrumbs and nuts.
4 Heat oil in large frying pan; shallow-fry fingers, in batches, until browned lightly and cooked through. Drain on absorbent paper.
5 Meanwhile, boil, steam or microwave peas until tender; drain. Coarsely crush peas with butter in medium bowl; stir in mint.
6 Serve fish fingers with mushy minted peas, and mayonnaise and lemon wedges, if you like.
nutritional count per serving 37.1g total fat (9g saturated fat); 3127kJ (748 cal); 33.5g carbohydrate; 66.7g protein; 6.9g fibre

There are many versions of this quintessential Italian recipe. You can prepare the schnitzel a day ahead – perfect for preparing on a Sunday night, ready to cook for a quick Monday night dinner.

VEAL SALTIMBOCCA

preparation time 15 minutes | cooking time 20 minutes | serves 4

1 Top each piece of veal with prosciutto, cheese, tomatoes and sage leaves. Fold in half to secure filling; secure with toothpicks or small skewers.
2 Melt half the butter in medium frying pan; cook veal, in batches, until cooked as desired. Cover to keep warm.
3 Add wine to same pan; bring to the boil. Boil, uncovered, until wine reduces by half. Stir in remaining butter, juice and sage.
4 Serve saltimbocca drizzled with sauce.
nutritional count per serving 24g total fat (13.1g saturated fat); 2312kJ (553 cal); 9g carbohydrate; 63.3g protein; 3.6g fibre

8 veal schnitzels (800g)
8 slices prosciutto (120g)
4 bocconcini cheese (240g), sliced thinly
⅔ cup (100g) drained semi-dried tomatoes
16 fresh sage leaves
40g butter
1 cup (250ml) dry white wine
1 tablespoon lemon juice
2 tablespoons coarsely chopped fresh sage

SALMON AND POTATO PATTIES WITH DILL CREAM SAUCE

preparation time 20 minutes (plus refrigeration time) | cooking time 30 minutes | serves 4

4 medium potatoes (800g), chopped coarsely
40g butter, softened
1 egg
½ cup (40g) finely grated parmesan cheese
415g can pink salmon
4 green onions, sliced thinly
1 clove garlic, crushed
½ cup (50g) packaged breadcrumbs
vegetable oil, for shallow-frying
200g green beans, trimmed
dill cream sauce
⅓ cup (80ml) dry white wine
300ml cream
1 tablespoon horseradish cream
2 teaspoons lemon juice
1 tablespoon finely chopped fresh dill

1 Boil, steam or microwave potato until tender; drain. Mash potato in large bowl with butter, egg and cheese until smooth.
2 Drain salmon; discard skin and bones, then flake into pieces. Add salmon, onion and garlic to potato mixture; mix well. Shape salmon mixture into 8 patties; coat in breadcrumbs. Place patties on oven tray. Cover; refrigerate 30 minutes.
3 Heat oil in large frying pan; shallow-fry patties, in batches, until browned lightly and heated through. Drain on absorbent paper.
4 Meanwhile, make dill cream sauce.
5 Boil, steam or microwave beans until tender; drain.
6 Serve patties with beans and dill cream sauce.
dill cream sauce Bring wine to the boil in small saucepan; boil, uncovered, until reduced by half. Add cream, horseradish cream and juice; cook, stirring, about 3 minutes or until sauce thickens slightly. Stir in dill.
nutritional count per serving 79.6g total fat (34.8g saturated fat); 4272kJ (1022 cal); 39.3g carbohydrate; 33.4g protein; 5.5g fibre

Horseradish cream is a commercially prepared creamy paste consisting of grated horseradish, vinegar, oil and sugar, while prepared horseradish is the preserved grated root. Both are available from supermarkets, so be sure to select the cream for this recipe.

We used perch fillets for this recipe, but any firm white fish fillet, such as bream, blue-eye or ling, can be used.

TEMPURA FISH & VEGIE CHIPS

preparation time 20 minutes (plus standing time) | cooking time 20 minutes | serves 4

1 cup (200g) rice flour
1¾ cups (260g) cornflour
1½ cups (375ml) chilled
    soda water
vegetable oil, for deep-frying
8 x 100g firm white fish fillets
2 baby eggplants (120g),
    cut into 1cm chips
1 medium red capsicum (200g),
    cut into 1cm chips
1 medium zucchini (120g),
    cut into 1cm chips
asian-style dipping sauce
⅓ cup (80ml) mirin
⅓ cup (80ml) japanese soy sauce
¼ cup (60ml) rice wine vinegar
2 tablespoons water
1 fresh small red thai chilli,
    chopped finely
1 clove garlic, crushed
2cm piece fresh ginger (10g),
    grated

1 Make dipping sauce.
2 Place rice flour, 1 cup of the cornflour and soda in medium bowl; stir until combined (mixture should be lumpy). Cover; stand 30 minutes.
3 Heat oil in wok. Coat fish and vegetables in remaining cornflour; shake off excess. Dip fish and vegetables in batter; deep-fry, in batches, until browned lightly and crisp. Drain on absorbent paper.
4 Serve tempura immediately with dipping sauce.
asian-style dipping sauce Combine ingredients in screw-top jar; shake well.
nutritional count per serving 17g total fat (2.2g saturated fat); 2483kJ (594 cal); 99.2g carbohydrate; 5.9g protein; 3.3g fibre

Baked risotto is a delicious alternative to the usual hand-stirred risotto (and a lot easier, too). Be sure to cover the risotto mixture tightly with foil while baking to ensure a perfectly creamy result.

BAKED ASPARAGUS RISOTTO

preparation time 20 minutes | cooking time 50 minutes | serves 4

1 Preheat oven to 180°C/160°C fan-forced.
2 Bring stock, rind and juice to the boil in medium saucepan. Reduce heat; simmer, covered.
3 Meanwhile, heat oil in medium saucepan; cook onion and garlic, stirring, until onion softens. Add rice; stir to coat in onion mixture. Stir in simmering stock mixture.
4 Place risotto mixture in shallow large ovenproof dish; cover with foil. Bake about 25 minutes, stirring halfway through cooking. Add asparagus and tomatoes; bake, uncovered, about 25 minutes or until rice is tender.
5 Remove from oven; sprinkle with cheese and thyme.
nutritional count per serving 8g total fat (2.5g saturated fat); 1262kJ (388 cal); 65.2g carbohydrate; 11.5g protein; 2.7g fibre

3½ cups (875ml) chicken or
  vegetable stock
2 teaspoons finely grated
  lemon rind
¼ cup (60ml) lemon juice
1 tablespoon olive oil
1 medium brown onion (150g),
  chopped finely
1 clove garlic, crushed
1½ cups (300g) arborio rice
170g asparagus, trimmed,
  cut into 3cm lengths
250g cherry tomatoes, halved
⅓ cup (25g) finely grated
  parmesan cheese
2 teaspoons finely chopped
  fresh thyme

You need to start this recipe a day ahead. Cook 1 cup (200g) white long-grain rice to make the required amount of cooked rice. You can add a couple of coarsely chopped bacon rashers to the recipe, if you like.

VEGETABLE AND OMELETTE FRIED RICE

preparation time 30 minutes (plus refrigeration time) | cooking time 15 minutes | serves 4

1 Spread rice, in thin layer, on shallow tray. Cover; refrigerate overnight.
2 Heat 1 teaspoon of the peanut oil in wok; cook half the egg over medium heat, swirling wok to form thin omelette. Remove from wok; cool. Repeat with another teaspoon of peanut oil and remaining egg. Roll omelettes tightly; cut into thin strips.
3 Heat remaining peanut oil in wok; stir-fry brown onion, garlic, ginger and chilli until onion softens. Add capsicum, carrot, beans and mushrooms; stir-fry until vegetables are tender. Add rice, sauces, sesame oil and five-spice; stir-fry until hot. Add sprouts and green onion; stir-fry until heated through.
4 Serve bowls of fried rice topped with omelette and nuts.

nutritional count per serving 15.2g total fat (2.9g saturated fat); 1697kJ (406 cal); 50.6g carbohydrate; 13.3g protein; 6.2g fibre

3 cups cooked
  white long-grain rice
1 tablespoon peanut oil
2 eggs, beaten lightly
1 medium brown onion (150g),
  sliced thickly
2 cloves garlic, crushed
3cm piece fresh ginger (15g),
  grated
1 fresh long red chilli,
  sliced thinly
1 medium red capsicum (200g),
  sliced thinly
1 medium carrot (120g),
  sliced thinly
100g green beans, trimmed,
  chopped coarsely
100g fresh shiitake mushrooms,
  sliced thinly
2 tablespoons light soy sauce
1 tablespoon oyster sauce
1 teaspoon sesame oil
1 teaspoon chinese five-spice
1 cup (80g) bean sprouts
4 green onions, sliced thinly
⅓ cup (50g) roasted unsalted
  cashews, chopped coarsely

APPLE AND PECAN STREUSEL MUFFINS

preparation time 20 minutes (plus freezing time)
cooking time 45 minutes | makes 12

4 medium apples (600g)
20g butter
⅓ cup (75g) firmly packed brown sugar
2 cups (300g) self-raising flour
¾ cup (165g) caster sugar
1 cup (120g) coarsely chopped roasted pecans
¾ cup (180ml) buttermilk
90g butter, melted
1 egg, beaten lightly
streusel topping
⅓ cup (50g) plain flour
2 tablespoons self-raising flour
¼ cup (55g) firmly packed brown sugar
½ teaspoon mixed spice
80g butter, chopped coarsely

1 Make streusel topping.
2 Preheat oven to 180°C/160°C fan-forced. Grease two x 6-hole ¾-cup (180ml) texas muffin pans.
3 Peel, core and quarter apples; slice thinly. Melt butter in large frying pan; cook apple, stirring, about 5 minutes or until browned lightly. Add brown sugar; cook, stirring, about 5 minutes or until mixture thickens slightly.
4 Sift flour into large bowl; stir in remaining ingredients (do not overmix; the batter should be lumpy).
5 Spoon mixture into pan holes; top with apple mixture. Coarsely grate streusel topping over muffins; bake about 35 minutes. Stand in pan 5 minutes; turn, top-side up, onto wire rack to cool.
streusel topping Process all ingredients until they come together. Enclose in plastic wrap; freeze about 1 hour or until firm.
nutritional count per serving 21.3g total fat (9.4g saturated fat); 1793kJ (429 cal); 52.5g carbohydrate; 5.5g protein; 2.7g fibre

CAKES, BISCUITS & SLICES

Instead of the apple, the same weight
of pear can be used in this recipe.
Muffins can be stored in an airtight
container for up to two days.

By spooning dollops of the almond coconut topping all over the slice, you will find it easier to spread evenly.

BERRY, ALMOND AND COCONUT SLICE

preparation time 25 minutes (plus cooling time) | cooking time 1 hour | serves 16

2 cups (300g) frozen
  mixed berries
1 cup (220g) caster sugar
1 tablespoon lime juice
90g butter, softened
1 egg
⅔ cup (100g) plain flour
¼ cup (35g) self-raising flour
1 tablespoon custard powder
almond coconut topping
2 eggs, beaten lightly
1½ cups (75g) flaked coconut
1 cup (80g) flaked almonds
¼ cup (55g) caster sugar

1 Preheat oven to 180°C/160°C fan-forced. Grease 20cm x 30cm lamington pan; line base with baking paper, extending paper 5cm over long sides.
2 Combine half the berries, half the sugar and the juice in small saucepan; stir over low heat until sugar dissolves. Bring to the boil; reduce heat. Simmer, uncovered, stirring occasionally, about 20 minutes or until mixture thickens; cool 10 minutes. Stir in remaining berries.
3 Beat butter, egg and remaining sugar in small bowl with electric mixer until light and fluffy; stir in sifted flours and custard powder. Spread dough into pan; spread with berry mixture.
4 Make almond coconut topping; sprinkle topping over berry mixture. Bake about 40 minutes; cool, then cut into 16 slices.
almond coconut topping Combine ingredients in small bowl.
nutritional count per serving 11.6g total fat (6.2g saturated fat); 932kJ (223 cal); 25g carbohydrate; 3.8g protein; 1.9g fibre

Cookies can be made up
to one week ahead: store
in an airtight container.
If you prefer, you can use
milk chocolate in place of the
dark chocolate in this recipe.

FUDGY CHOCOLATE, CHERRY
AND COCONUT COOKIES

preparation time 20 minutes | cooking time 10 minutes | makes 36

125g butter, softened
¾ cup (165g) firmly packed
   brown sugar
1 egg
1 teaspoon vanilla extract
1 cup (150g) plain flour
¼ cup (35g) self-raising flour
⅓ cup (35g) cocoa powder
½ teaspoon bicarbonate of soda
½ cup (125ml) milk
4 x 55g Cherry Ripe chocolate
   bars, cut into 1cm pieces
100g dark eating chocolate,
   cut into 1cm pieces

1 Preheat oven to 180°C/160°C fan-forced. Grease three oven trays;
line with baking paper.
2 Beat butter, sugar, egg and extract in medium bowl with electric mixer
until smooth. Stir in sifted flours, cocoa and soda with milk in two batches;
stir in chocolate pieces.
3 Drop level tablespoons of mixture, about 5cm apart, onto trays; press
with fork to flatten slightly. Bake about 10 minutes. Stand cookies 5 minutes
before transferring to wire rack to cool.
nutritional count per cookie 5.5g total fat (3.6g saturated fat); 460kJ
(110 cal); 13.5g carbohydrate; 1.5g protein; 0.6g fibre

Dried sweetened cranberries have the same slightly sour, succulent flavour as fresh cranberries, but with the addition of a sweetener. They are available from supermarkets.

WHITE CHOCOLATE, CRANBERRY AND PISTACHIO HEDGEHOG SLICE

preparation time 10 minutes (plus refrigeration time) | cooking time 5 minutes | serves 12

1 Grease 8cm x 26cm bar pan; line base with baking paper, extending paper 5cm over long sides.
2 Stir condensed milk and butter in small saucepan over low heat until smooth. Remove from heat; add chocolate, stir until smooth.
3 Break biscuits into small pieces; place in large bowl with cranberries and nuts. Stir in chocolate mixture.
4 Spread mixture into pan, cover; refrigerate about 3 hours or overnight until firm. Cut into 12 slices.
nutritional count per serving 14.9g total fat (8.2g saturated fat); 1179kJ (282 cal); 32.3g carbohydrate; 4.4g protein; 0.9g fibre

¾ cup (180ml) sweetened condensed milk
60g butter, chopped
180g white eating chocolate, chopped coarsely
150g plain sweet biscuits
½ cup (65g) dried cranberries
⅓ cup (45g) roasted unsalted pistachios

CHOC-MINT BROWNIES

preparation time 15 minutes (plus refrigeration time) | cooking time 30 minutes | makes 18

200g dark eating chocolate, melted
125g butter, chopped coarsely
200g dark eating chocolate,
    chopped coarsely
½ cup (110g) caster sugar
2 eggs
1¼ cups (185g) plain flour
6 mint patties (120g),
    chopped coarsely

1 Preheat oven to 180°C/160°C fan-forced. Grease deep 19cm-square cake pan; line base with baking paper, extending paper 5cm over sides. Line base with foil.
2 Spread melted chocolate evenly over base of pan; cover, refrigerate until set.
3 Meanwhile, combine butter and chopped chocolate in medium saucepan; stir over low heat until smooth. Remove from heat; stir in sugar. Cool 10 minutes.
4 Stir in eggs, then sifted flour and mint patties. Spread mixture over chocolate in pan. Bake about 30 minutes. Cool in pan; refrigerate about 30 minutes to set chocolate again. Turn brownie, chocolate-side up, onto board; carefully peel foil from chocolate topping.
5 Cut brownie into 9 squares; cut squares in half diagonally.
nutritional count per brownie 14.1g total fat (8.8g saturated fat); 1116kJ (267 cal); 31.4g carbohydrate; 3.3g protein; 0.7g fibre

Brownies can be frozen for up to three months in an airtight container.

You need two large overripe bananas (460g) to get the amount of mashed banana needed for this recipe. For the authentic café experience, lightly toast the banana bread and serve it with butter.

BANANA BREAD

preparation time 20 minutes | cooking time 1 hour | serves 12

1 cup mashed banana
1 cup (220g) firmly packed
    dark brown sugar
2 eggs, beaten lightly
40g butter, melted
½ cup (125ml) buttermilk
¼ cup (90g) treacle
1½ cups (225g) plain flour
1 cup (150g) self-raising flour
2 teaspoons mixed spice
1 teaspoon bicarbonate of soda

1 Preheat oven to 180°C/160°C fan-forced. Grease 14cm x 21cm loaf pan; line base and long sides with baking paper, extending paper 5cm over sides.
2 Combine banana, sugar, egg, butter, buttermilk and treacle in large bowl; stir in sifted dry ingredients (do not overmix; the batter should be lumpy). Spoon mixture into pan.
3 Bake about 1 hour. Stand in pan 10 minutes; turn, top-side up, onto wire rack to cool.
nutritional count per serving 4.2g total fat (2.3g saturated fat); 1099kJ (263 cal); 49.5g carbohydrate; 5.3g protein; 1.7g fibre

This cake can be stored at room temperature in an airtight container for two days; un-iced cake can be frozen for up to two months.

CHERRY AND SULTANA BUTTER CAKE WITH COCONUT FROSTING

preparation time 30 minutes | cooking time 1 hour | serves 12

1 Preheat oven to 180°C/160°C fan-forced. Grease deep 22cm-round cake pan; line with baking paper.
2 Beat butter, extract and sugar in medium bowl with electric mixer until light and fluffy. Beat in eggs, one at a time. Stir in sifted flours and milk, in two batches. Stir in sultanas and cherries.
3 Spread mixture into pan; bake about 1 hour. Stand 5 minutes; turn, top-side up, onto wire rack to cool.
4 Meanwhile, make coconut frosting. Top cake with coconut frosting.
coconut frosting Sift icing sugar into medium bowl; stir in coconut and egg white until combined; tint lightly with pink colouring.
nutritional count per serving 22.3g total fat (14.8g saturated fat); 2144kJ (513 cal); 70.7g carbohydrate; 5.9g protein; 2.5g fibre

250g butter, softened
1 teaspoon vanilla extract
1 cup (220g) caster sugar
3 eggs
1¼ cups (185g) plain flour
1 cup (150g) self-raising flour
⅓ cup (80ml) milk
1 cup (160g) sultanas
¾ cup (150g) coarsely chopped
    red glacé cherries
coconut frosting
1 cup (160g) icing sugar
¾ cup (60g) desiccated coconut
1 egg white
pink food colouring

PISTACHIO ORANGE PIE

preparation time 20 minutes (plus refrigeration time)
cooking time 1 hour | serves 10

1⅓ cups (185g) coarsely chopped unsalted pistachios
1 tablespoon plain flour
2 tablespoons brown sugar
40g butter, melted
2 eggs
¾ cup (180ml) maple syrup
2 teaspoons finely grated orange rind
1 tablespoon orange juice
2 tablespoons orange marmalade, warmed, sieved
pastry
1¼ cups (185g) plain flour
⅓ cup (55g) icing sugar
125g cold butter, chopped coarsely
1 egg yolk
1 teaspoon iced water, approximately

1 Make pastry.
2 Grease 24cm-round loose-based flan tin. Roll pastry between sheets of baking paper until large enough to line tin. Ease pastry into tin, press into base and side; trim edge. Cover; refrigerate 30 minutes.
3 Preheat oven to 180°C/160°C fan-forced.
4 Place tin on oven tray. Line pastry case with baking paper; fill with dried beans or rice. Bake 10 minutes; remove paper and beans carefully from pie shell. Bake 5 minutes; cool.
5 Reduce temperature to 160°C/140°C fan-forced.
6 Combine nuts, flour, sugar, butter, eggs, syrup, rind and juice in medium bowl. Pour mixture into pastry case.
7 Bake about 45 minutes. Cool. Brush pie with marmalade.
pastry Process flour, icing sugar and butter until crumbly. Add egg yolk and enough of the water to process until ingredients come together. Knead dough on floured surface until smooth. Cover; refrigerate 30 minutes.
nutritional count per serving 23.7g total fat (10.2g saturated fat); 1785kJ (427 cal); 44.9g carbohydrate; 7.4g protein; 2.5g fibre

DESSERTS

DOUBLE CHOCOLATE MOUSSE

preparation time 30 minutes (plus refrigeration time) | cooking time 15 minutes | serves 6

100g dark eating chocolate,
   chopped coarsely
10g unsalted butter,
   chopped coarsely
1 egg, separated
½ cup (125ml) thickened cream,
   whipped
1 cup (250ml) thickened cream,
   whipped, extra
milk chocolate mousse
100g milk eating chocolate,
   chopped coarsely
10g unsalted butter,
   chopped coarsely
1 egg, separated
½ cup (125ml) thickened cream,
   whipped

1 Melt chocolate in small heatproof bowl over small saucepan of simmering water. Remove from heat; add butter, stir until smooth. Stir in egg yolk.
2 Beat egg white in small bowl with electric mixer until soft peaks form. Fold egg white and cream into chocolate mixture, in two batches.
3 Make milk chocolate mousse.
4 Divide dark chocolate mousse among six ¾-cup (180ml) serving glasses; top with milk chocolate mousse then extra whipped cream. Cover; refrigerate 3 hours or overnight.
milk chocolate mousse Repeat steps 1 and 2, using milk chocolate in place of dark chocolate.
nutritional count per serving 43.9g total fat (28.1g saturated fat); 2128kJ (509 cal); 23.5g carbohydrate; 6.1g protein; 0.3g fibre

For an easy dessert to serve at a party,
make the mousse in shot glasses or liqueur
glasses. Serve topped with fresh berries
and chocolate curls for an elegant look.

Although homemade lemon curd is divine, you can use store-bought lemon curd if you're short of time. Sponge cakes and meringues are also available, already prepared, from most supermarkets.

LEMON CURD, BLUEBERRY AND MERINGUE TRIFLE

preparation time 30 minutes (plus refrigeration and cooling time) | cooking time 20 minutes | serves 6

2 cups (500ml) grape juice
85g packet blueberry jelly crystals
200g sponge cake,
  cut into 3cm pieces
¼ cup (60ml) sweet sherry
2 teaspoons finely grated
  lemon rind
¾ cup (180ml) lemon juice
1 cup (220g) caster sugar
4 eggs
80g butter, chopped coarsely
1 teaspoon gelatine
1 tablespoon water
300ml thickened cream
50g meringue, chopped coarsely
2 cups (300g) fresh blueberries

1 Bring grape juice to the boil in small saucepan; stir in jelly crystals until dissolved. Pour jelly mixture into shallow container. Refrigerate about 20 minutes or until jelly is almost set.
2 Place cake in 3-litre (12-cup) bowl; sprinkle with sherry.
3 Combine rind, juice, sugar, eggs and butter in medium heatproof bowl. Place over medium saucepan of simmering water; cook, stirring, about 15 minutes or until curd coats the back of a spoon.
4 Sprinkle gelatine over the water in small heatproof jug. Stand jug in small saucepan of simmering water; stir until gelatine dissolves. Stir gelatine mixture into warm lemon curd. Cool to room temperature.
5 Pour jelly over cake; refrigerate 15 minutes. Top with lemon curd. Cover; refrigerate 3 hours or overnight.
6 Just before serving, beat cream in small bowl with electric mixer until soft peaks form; spread over curd. Sprinkle with meringue and berries.
nutritional count per serving 34.7g total fat (21g saturated fat); 3168kJ (758 cal); 97.5g carbohydrate; 10.6g protein; 1.3g fibre

Any type of berries, fresh or frozen, can be used instead of the raspberries in this pudding. If you prefer, use dark or milk eating chocolate in place of the white chocolate. Sprinkle the pudding with icing sugar and serve with a good quality ice-cream for a truly indulgent dessert.

WHITE CHOCOLATE AND RASPBERRY CROISSANT PUDDING

preparation time 15 minutes | cooking time 1 hour | serves 8

1 Preheat oven to 160°C/140°C fan-forced.
2 Make custard.
3 Grease shallow 2-litre (8-cup) ovenproof dish. Layer croissant slices, overlapping slightly, in dish; dollop spoonfuls of jam over slices. Sprinkle with chocolate and berries. Pour custard over the top.
4 Place dish in large baking dish; add enough boiling water to come halfway up sides of ovenproof dish. Bake about 1 hour or until pudding sets. Remove pudding from baking dish; stand 5 minutes before serving.
custard Combine cream, milk, sugar and extract in medium saucepan; bring to the boil. Whisk eggs in large bowl; whisking constantly, gradually add hot milk mixture to egg mixture.
nutritional count per serving 37.5g total fat (22.7g saturated fat); 2328kJ (557 cal); 44g carbohydrate; 10.4g protein; 2.2g fibre

5 croissants (300g), sliced thinly
⅓ cup (110g) raspberry jam
100g white eating chocolate, chopped coarsely
1 cup (135g) raspberries
custard
1½ cups (375ml) cream
1¼ cups (310ml) milk
⅓ cup (75g) caster sugar
1 teaspoon vanilla extract
4 eggs

Instead of making 8 pancakes, you can use this recipe to make 24 pikelets. Follow the recipe, using one tablespoon of batter for each pikelet, at step 2.

PANCAKES

preparation time 5 minutes | cooking time 20 minutes | serves 4

1 cup (150g) self-raising flour
¼ cup (55g) caster sugar
2 eggs
1 cup (250ml) milk

1 Sift flour and sugar into medium bowl; gradually whisk in combined eggs and milk until batter is smooth.
2 Pour ¼ cup batter into heated oiled medium frying pan; cook pancake until bubbles begin to appear on surface. Turn pancake; cook until browned lightly. Cover to keep warm.
3 Repeat with remaining batter.
4 Serve pancakes with your choice of topping.
nutritional count per pancake 1.4g total fat (0.8g saturated fat); 502kJ (120 cal); 21.7g carbohydrate; 4.4g protein; 0.7g fibre

TOPPINGS
rhubarb and pear Combine 2 cups coarsely chopped rhubarb, 1 coarsely chopped medium pear, ¼ cup caster sugar, 2 tablespoons water and 1 teaspoon mixed spice in medium saucepan; bring to the boil. Reduce heat; simmer, stirring occasionally, about 5 minutes or until fruit softens slightly.
nutritional count per serving 0.2g total fat (0g saturated fat); 380kJ (91 cal); 19.8g carbohydrate; 1g protein; 2.7g fibre

orange-glazed strawberries Combine ¼ cup water and ¼ cup caster sugar in small saucepan; stir over low heat until sugar dissolves. Bring to the boil; boil, uncovered, about 3 minutes or until syrup thickens slightly. Stir in 2 teaspoons finely grated orange rind and 1 tablespoon orange juice; cool. Stir in 250g quartered strawberries and ¼ cup coarsely chopped fresh mint.
nutritional count per serving 0.1g total fat (0g saturated fat); 301kJ (72 cal); 15.5g carbohydrate; 1.2g protein; 1.7g fibre

chocolate, banana and hazelnut Combine 100g coarsely chopped milk eating chocolate, 10g butter and ½ cup cream in small saucepan; stir over low heat until smooth. Drizzle chocolate sauce over pancakes; top with 2 thinly sliced medium bananas and ¼ cup coarsely chopped roasted hazelnuts.
nutritional count per serving 27.8g total fat (14.7g saturated fat); 1588kJ (380 cal); 29.9g carbohydrate; 4.9g protein; 2.3g fibre

If the pavlova "crust" does not lift off, you can split the pavlova in half horizontally. Spread half the cream and fruit over the base then top with remaining pavlova, cream and fruit. Or, simply cover top and sides of pavlova with the cream and decorate the top with the fruit. Feel free to use whatever fruit is in season – mango and raspberries look and taste great on a pavlova.

EASY PAVLOVA

preparation time 25 minutes (plus cooling time) | cooking time 1 hour 45 minutes | serves 12

6 egg whites
1½ cups (330g) caster sugar
1 tablespoon cornflour
1 teaspoon vanilla extract
1 teaspoon white vinegar
300ml thickened cream
1 tablespoon icing sugar
1 cup (150g) blueberries
125g strawberries, sliced thinly
1 medium kiwifruit (85g), halved, sliced thinly
¼ cup (60ml) passionfruit pulp

1 Preheat oven to 120°C/100°C fan-forced. Grease 22cm-round springform tin; line base and side with baking paper.
2 Beat egg whites in medium bowl with electric mixer until soft peaks form; gradually add caster sugar, one tablespoon at a time, beating until sugar dissolves between additions. Fold in cornflour, extract and vinegar.
3 Spread mixture into tin; bake about 1¾ hours. Cool pavlova in oven with door ajar.
4 Meanwhile, beat cream and icing sugar in small bowl with electric mixer until firm peaks form.
5 Remove pavlova from tin; peel baking paper from side. Carefully lift top crust from pavlova; set aside. Spread pavlova with half the cream; top with half the berries and half the kiwifruit. Place crust back on top of pavlova; top with remaining cream, berries and kiwifruit. Drizzle with passionfruit.
6 Serve pavlova dusted with extra sifted icing sugar.
nutritional count per serving 9.3g total fat (6.1g saturated fat); 957kJ (229 cal); 32.6g carbohydrate; 2.8g protein; 1.4g fibre

Pecans can be used in place
of the walnuts, if you prefer.
Be careful when measuring
the bicarb – any extra, and
you will taste its distinct,
bitter flavour in the pudding.

TOFFEE DATE AND GINGER PUDDINGS

preparation time 30 minutes | cooking time 30 minutes | makes 6

1 Preheat oven to 160°C/140°C fan-forced. Grease six-hole ¾-cup (180ml) texas muffin pan; line bases with baking paper.
2 Combine glacé ginger and nuts in small bowl; sprinkle mixture over bases of pan holes.
3 Combine dates and the water in small saucepan; bring to the boil. Remove from heat; stir in soda. Stand 5 minutes.
4 Blend or process date mixture with butter and sugar until smooth. Add eggs, flour and ground ginger; process until combined.
5 Pour mixture into pan holes; bake about 30 minutes. Stand 5 minutes; turn onto wire rack to cool 5 minutes.
6 Meanwhile, make ginger butterscotch sauce.
7 Serve warm puddings drizzled with ginger butterscotch sauce.
ginger butterscotch sauce Stir ingredients in small saucepan over low heat until smooth. Simmer, uncovered, 5 minutes.
nutritional count per serving 41g total fat (22.1g saturated fat); 3035kJ (726 cal); 81.1g carbohydrate; 6.7g protein; 3.7g fibre

½ cup (115g) finely chopped
    glacé ginger
½ cup (60g) finely chopped
    roasted walnuts
1 cup (140g) seeded dried dates
¾ cup (180ml) water
1 teaspoon bicarbonate of soda
50g butter, chopped coarsely
½ cup (110g) firmly packed
    brown sugar
2 eggs
¾ cup (110g) self-raising flour
1 teaspoon ground ginger
ginger butterscotch sauce
½ cup (110g) firmly packed
    brown sugar
⅔ cup (160ml) cream
100g butter, chopped coarsely
½ teaspoon ground ginger

Serve the fritters with coconut ice-cream. To make your own, soften 1-litre of good-quality vanilla ice-cream, then fold in 1 cup toasted shredded coconut and ¼ cup coconut-flavoured liqueur. Return to the freezer until firm enough to scoop.

If you can't find japanese breadcrumbs, combine ½ cup stale white breadcrumbs and ¼ cup packaged breadcrumbs and use these instead; the taste and texture of the fritters, however, won't be the same.

BANANA FRITTERS

preparation time 10 minutes | cooking time 20 minutes | serves 4

¼ cup (40g) icing sugar
2 teaspoons ground cinnamon
1 egg, beaten lightly
¾ cup (50g) japanese
   breadcrumbs
vegetable oil, for deep-frying
4 large bananas (920g),
   halved lengthways

1 Combine sugar and cinnamon in shallow medium bowl. Beat egg in shallow medium bowl; place breadcrumbs in another bowl.
2 Heat oil in medium saucepan.
3 Meanwhile, dip bananas in sugar mixture: shake off excess. Dip banana in egg, then in crumbs to coat.
4 Deep-fry bananas, in batches, until browned. Drain on absorbent paper.
nutritional count per serving 9.7g total fat (1.5g saturated fat); 1329kJ (318 cal); 49.2g carbohydrate; 6g protein; 3.9g fibre

Serve warm apple pie slice with ice-cream or whipped cream. Ground nutmeg or cinnamon tastes great stirred through the ice-cream or cream.

APPLE PIE SLICE

preparation time 20 minutes (plus refrigeration time) | cooking time 25 minutes | serves 8

1 Make apple filling.

2 Grease 20cm x 30cm lamington pan; line base with baking paper, extending paper 5cm over long sides.

3 Sift flours into medium bowl, rub in butter. Stir in sugar, egg and enough milk to make a firm dough. Knead on floured surface until smooth. Cover; refrigerate 30 minutes.

4 Preheat oven to 200°C/180°C fan-forced.

5 Divide dough in half. Roll one half large enough to cover base of pan; press firmly into pan. Spread apple filling over dough. Roll remaining dough large enough to cover filling and place over the top. Brush with extra milk; sprinkle with extra sugar. Bake about 25 minutes; stand in pan 5 minutes.

apple filling Combine apple, sugar and the water in large saucepan; cook, uncovered, stirring occasionally, about 10 minutes or until apple softens. Remove from heat; stir in sultanas, spice and rind. Cool.

nutritional count per serving 9.7g total fat (5.9g saturated fat); 1463kJ (350 cal); 58.6g carbohydrate; 4.8g protein; 3.4g fibre

1 cup (150g) self-raising flour
½ cup (75g) plain flour
80g cold butter, chopped coarsely
¼ cup (55g) caster sugar
1 egg, beaten lightly
¼ cup (60ml) milk, approximately
1 tablespoon milk, extra
1 tablespoon caster sugar, extra
apple filling
6 medium apples (900g), peeled, cored, cut into 1cm pieces
¼ cup (55g) caster sugar
¼ cup (60ml) water
¾ cup (120g) sultanas
1 teaspoon mixed spice
2 teaspoons finely grated lemon rind

AÏOLI home-made garlic mayonnaise traditionally from the south of France.

BEANS

borlotti also known as roman beans or pink beans; can be eaten fresh or dried. Interchangeable with pinto beans because of the similarity in appearance – both are pale pink or beige with dark red streaks. The bean of choice for frijoles refritos (refried beans).

four-bean mix combination of kidney beans, butter beans, chickpeas and cannellini beans.

kidney medium-sized red bean, slightly floury in texture yet sweet in flavour; sold dried or canned. It's found in bean mixes and is the bean used in chilli con carne.

sprouts also known as bean shoots; tender new growths of assorted beans and seeds germinated for consumption. The most readily available are mung beans, soy beans, alfalfa and snow pea sprouts.

BICARBONATE OF SODA also known as baking or carb soda; used as a leavening agent in baking.

BROCCOLINI a cross between broccoli and chinese kale; milder and sweeter than broccoli. Each long stem is topped by a loose floret that closely resembles broccoli; from floret to stem, broccolini is completely edible.

BURGHUL also known as bulghur or bulgar wheat; hulled steamed wheat kernels that, once dried, are crushed into various-sized grains. Not the same as cracked wheat. Used in Middle-Eastern dishes such as kibbeh and tabbouleh. Found in most supermarkets or health-food stores.

BUTTERMILK originally the term given to the slightly sour liquid left after butter was churned from cream, today it is commercially made similarly to yogurt. Sold alongside all fresh milk products in supermarkets; despite the implication of its name, it is low in fat.

CHEESE

bocconcini means mouthful; a walnut-sized, fresh, baby mozzarella. Is a delicate, semi-soft, white cheese traditionally made from buffalo milk. Spoils rapidly so must be kept under refrigeration, in brine, for one or two days at most.

fetta a crumbly goat- or sheep-milk cheese with a sharp salty taste.

mozzarella a soft, spun-curd cheese. It has a low melting point and wonderfully elastic texture when heated, and is used to add texture rather than flavour.

parmesan also known as parmigiana; a hard, grainy cows-milk cheese. The curd is salted in brine for a month before being aged for up to two years in humid conditions.

pizza a commercial blend of processed grated mozzarella, cheddar and parmesan.

ricotta the name roughly translates as "cooked again". It is a soft, white, sweet, moist cows-milk cheese made from whey, a by-product of other cheese-making, to which fresh milk and acid are added.

CHERRY RIPE confectionary made from chocolate, coconut, sugar, cherries, glucose and milk powder.

CHICKPEAS also called channa, garbanzos or hummus; a sandy-coloured, irregularly round legume.

CHILLIES always use rubber gloves when seeding and chopping fresh chillies as they can burn your skin. We use unseeded chillies in our recipes because the seeds contain the heat; use fewer chillies rather than seeding the lot.

CHINESE BARBECUED DUCK traditionally cooked in special ovens, this duck has a sweet-sticky coating made from soy sauce, sherry, five-spice and hoisin sauce. It is available from Asian food stores.

CHINESE BARBECUE PORK also called char siew. Traditionally cooked in special ovens, this pork has a sweet-sticky coating made from soy sauce, sherry, five-spice powder and hoisin sauce. Available from Asian food stores.

COCOA POWDER also known as cocoa; dried, roasted then ground unsweetened cocoa beans.

COCONUT

cream obtained commercially from the first pressing of the coconut flesh, without the addition of water. Available in cans and cartons at supermarkets.

milk not the liquid found inside the fruit (which is called coconut water), but the diluted liquid from the second pressing of the white flesh of a mature coconut.

COUSCOUS a fine, grain-like cereal product made from semolina. A semolina flour and water dough is sieved then dehydrated to produce minuscule even-sized pellets; it is rehydrated by steaming, or with the addition of a warm liquid, and swells to three or four times its original size.

CROISSANT the French word for crescent. A rich, flaky pastry breakfast roll shaped like a crescent with a crisp texture on the outside, and a flaky layered, soft buttery centre.

DILL PICKLE a small cucumber preserved in a brine or vinegar flavoured with dill seed.

EGGPLANT also known as aubergine; actually a fruit and belongs to the same family as the tomato, chilli and potato. Ranging in size from tiny to very large and in colour from pale green to deep purple. Can be purchased char-grilled in jars.

FIVE-SPICE POWDER a fragrant mixture of ground cinnamon, cloves, star anise, sichuan pepper and fennel seeds. Also known as chinese five-spice.

FLOUR

cornflour also known as cornstarch; used as a thickening agent in cooking.

plain an all-purpose flour, made from wheat.

rice a very fine, almost powdery, gluten-free flour; made from ground white rice.

self-raising plain flour sifted with baking powder in the proportion of 1 cup flour to 2 teaspoons baking powder.

GLACÉ FRUIT cooked in heavy sugar syrup then dried.

GRAVY BEEF boneless stewing beef cut from the shin; slow-cooked, it imbues stocks, soups and casseroles with a gelatine richness. Cut crossways, with the bone in, it is called osso buco.

GREEN CURRY PASTE a prepared hot paste of chillies, garlic, onion, lemon grass, spice, salt and galangal.

JAPANESE BREADCRUMBS also known as panko. Available as large pieces or fine crumbs; have a lighter texture than Western-style breadcrumbs. Available from Asian grocery stores. Unless you make coarse breadcrumbs from white bread that's either quite stale or gently toasted, nothing is an adequate substitution. Gives a crunchy texture with a delicate, pale golden colour.

GLOSSARY

KIPFLER POTATOES small, finger-shaped potato with a nutty flavour.

KITCHEN STRING made from a natural product such as cotton or hemp that will neither melt nor affect the flavour of the food during cooking as would a string made from synthetic materials.

KUMARA the polynesian name of an orange-fleshed sweet potato often confused with yam.

LAMINGTON PAN 20cm x 30cm slab cake pan, 3cm deep.

LEEKS a member of the onion family, the leek resembles a green onion but is much larger and more subtle in flavour. Tender baby or pencil leeks can be eaten whole with minimal cooking; adult leeks must be trimmed then chopped or sliced before being cooked. Wash well before use.

LEMON PEPPER SEASONING a seasoning commercially made from a blend of crushed black pepper, lemon, herbs and spices; found on supermarket shelves.

LETTUCE
butter have small, round, loosely formed heads with soft, buttery-textured leaves ranging from pale green on the outer leaves to pale yellow-green on the inner leaves. Has a sweet flavour.
cos also known as romaine lettuce; the traditional caesar salad lettuce. Long, with leaves ranging from dark green on the outside to almost white near the core; the leaves have a stiff centre rib that gives a slight cupping effect to the leaf.

MINT PATTIE a soft, round, mint-flavoured confectionary covered with chocolate.

MIRIN Japanese champagne-coloured cooking wine; made of glutinous rice and alcohol and used expressly for cooking. Should not be confused with sake; there is also a seasoned sweet mirin called manjo mirin that is made of water, rice, corn syrup and alcohol.

MUSHROOMS
button small, cultivated white mushrooms with a mild flavour.
dried porcini also known as cèpes. They are expensive, but due to their strong nutty flavour, only small amounts are required for most dishes. Must be rehydrated before use.

enoki clumps of long, spaghetti-like stems with tiny, snowy white caps.
flat large, flat mushrooms with a rich earthy flavour; ideal for filling and barbecuing. They are sometimes misnamed field mushrooms, which are wild mushrooms.
oyster also known as abalone; a grey-white mushroom shaped like a fan. Prized for their smooth texture and subtle, oyster-like flavour.
shiitake when fresh are known as chinese black, forest or golden oak mushrooms; although cultivated they have the earthiness and taste of wild mushrooms. Are large and meaty. When dried, they are also known as donko or dried chinese mushrooms; rehydrate before use.
swiss brown also known as cremini or roman mushrooms; are light brown mushrooms having a full-bodied flavour. Button or cup mushrooms can be substituted for swiss browns.

MUSTARD
dijon pale brown, distinctively flavoured, fairly mild tasting french mustard.
wholegrain also known as seeded. Made from crushed mustard seeds and dijon-style french mustard. A course-grain mustard.

NOODLES
hokkien also known as stir-fry noodles; fresh wheat noodles resembling thick, yellow-brown spaghetti needing no pre-cooking before being used.
rice stick an especially popular South-East Asian dried rice noodle. Comes in different widths (thin, used in soups; and wide, used in stir-fries). Soak in hot water until soft.
rice vermicelli also known as sen mee, mei fun or bee hoon. Long thin noodles made with rice flour. Before using, soak in hot water until softened, boil them briefly then rinse with hot water.
singapore pre-cooked wheat noodles best described as a thinner version of hokkien.

OIL
cooking spray we use a cholesterol-free cooking spray made from canola oil.
olive made from ripened olives. Extra virgin and virgin are the best, while extra light or light refers to taste not fat levels.
peanut pressed from ground peanuts; most commonly used oil in Asian cooking because of its high smoke point (capacity to handle high heat without burning).

sesame made from roasted, crushed, white sesame seeds; a flavouring rather than a cooking medium.
vegetable sourced from plants rather than animal fats.

ONIONS
green also known as scallion or, incorrectly, shallot; an immature onion picked before the bulb has formed, having a long, bright-green edible stalk.
red also known as spanish, red spanish or bermuda onion; a sweet-flavoured, large, purple-red onion.
shallots also called french shallots, golden shallots or eschalots. Small, elongated, brown-skinned members of the onion family; they grow in tight clusters similar to garlic.
spring crisp, narrow green-leafed tops and a round sweet white bulb larger than that of green onions.

PANCETTA an Italian unsmoked bacon; pork belly is cured in salt and spices then rolled into a sausage shape and dried for several weeks. Bacon can be substituted.

PARSLEY, FLAT-LEAF also known as continental or italian parsley.

PARSNIP a long, white root vegetable with feathery green leaves. It is related to the carrot, which it resembles, although it has a paler colour and a stronger flavour.

PATTY-PAN SQUASH also known as crookneck or custard marrow pumpkins; a round, slightly flat summer squash being yellow to pale green in colour and having a scalloped edge. Harvested young, it has a firm white flesh and distinct flavour.

PIMIENTO-STUFFED GREEN OLIVE a green olive with a lively, briny bitterness containing a morsel of capsicum, which adds a flash of colour.

PLAIN SWEET BISCUITS also known as cookies; a crisp sweet biscuit without icing or any fillings.

POLENTA also known as cornmeal; a flour-like cereal made of dried corn (maize) and sold ground in different textures. Also the name of the dish made from it.

PROSCIUTTO a kind of unsmoked Italian ham; salted, air-cured and aged, it is usually eaten uncooked.

RICE

arborio a small, round-grain rice, well-suited to absorb a large amount of liquid; especially suitable for risottos.

long-grain an elongated grain that remains separate when cooked; the most popular steaming rice in Asia.

ROCKET also known as arugula, rugula and rucola; a peppery-tasting green leaf that can be used similarly to baby spinach leaves. Baby rocket leaves are both smaller and less peppery.

SAUCES

char siu a Chinese barbecue sauce made from sugar, water, salt, fermented soy bean paste, honey, soy sauce, malt syrup and spices. It can be found at most supermarkets.

fish also called nam pla or nuoc nam; made from pulverised salted fermented fish, most often anchovies. Has a pungent smell and strong taste; use sparingly.

hoisin a thick, sweet and spicy Chinese paste made from salted fermented soy beans, onions and garlic.

oyster Asian in origin, this rich, brown sauce is made from oysters and their brine, cooked with salt and soy sauce, and thickened with starches.

plum a thick, sweet and sour dipping sauce made from plums, vinegar, sugar, chillies and spices.

soy made from fermented soy beans. Several variations are available in most supermarkets and Asian food stores. *Dark soy* is a deep brown, almost black colour; rich, with a thicker consistency than the other types, and pungent, but not particularly salty. *Japanese soy* is an all-purpose low-sodium soy sauce made with more wheat content than its Chinese counterparts. Possibly the best table soy and the one to choose if you only want one variety. *Light soy* is a fairly thin, pale and salty tasting sauce; used in dishes in which the natural colour of the ingredients is to be maintained. Not to be confused with salt-reduced or low-sodium soy sauces.

sweet chilli a comparatively mild sauce made from red chillies, sugar, garlic and vinegar.

tomato also known as ketchup or catsup; is made from tomatoes, vinegar and spices.

worcestershire a dark coloured condiment usually made from garlic, soy sauce, lime, tamarind, onions, molasses, anchovies, vinegar and seasonings.

SHALLOT *see onions.*

SILVER BEET also known as swiss chard and, incorrectly, spinach.

SNOW PEAS also called mange tout; a variety of garden pea, eaten pod and all (though you may need to trim the ends). Snow pea sprouts are available from supermarkets or greengrocers and are usually eaten raw in salads or sandwiches.

SPATCHCOCK a small chicken (poussin), no more than six weeks old, weighing a maximum 500g. Also a cooking technique where a small chicken is split open, then flattened and grilled.

SPINACH also known as english spinach and, incorrectly, silver beet. Baby spinach leaves are best eaten raw.

STOCK available in tetra packs, bottles or cans. Stock cubes or powder can be used. As a guide, 1 teaspoon of stock powder or 1 small crumbled stock cube mixed with 1 cup (250ml) water will give a fairly strong stock. Be aware of the salt and fat content of stock cubes, powders and prepared stocks.

SUGAR

brown a very soft, finely granulated sugar retaining molasses for its characteristic colour and flavour. Dark brown sugar may be substituted.

caster also known as superfine or finely granulated table sugar.

icing sugar also known as confectioners' sugar or powdered sugar; granulated sugar crushed together with a small amount of cornflour.

palm sugar also known as nam tan pip, jaggery, jawa or gula melaka; made from the sap of the sugar palm tree. Light brown to black in colour and usually sold in rock-hard cakes. Substitute it with brown sugar, if unavailable.

white a coarse, granulated table sugar also known as crystal sugar.

SUGAR SNAP PEAS also known as honey snap peas; eaten whole, pod and all.

SWEET SHERRY a fortified wine.

SWEETENED CONDENSED MILK from which 60 per cent of the water has been removed; the remaining milk is then sweetened with sugar.

SWISS ROLL PAN also known as a jelly-roll pan; measures 26cm x 32cm. Its slightly raised sides help contain the mixture being baked, preventing the mixture from rising.

TARRAGON an aromatic herb with an anise-like flavour; available fresh, dried and powdered. To store, place fresh tarragon in a plastic bag with a damp paper towel; place in refrigerator, or place the stems in a glass of water and put a plastic bag over the top.

TOMATOES

cherry also known as tiny tim or tom thumb tomatoes; small and round.

egg also called plum or roma, these are smallish, oval-shaped tomatoes much used in Italian cooking or salads.

grape small, long, oval-shaped tomatoes.

TREACLE thick, dark syrup not unlike molasses; a by-product of sugar refining.

VANILLA

bean dried, long, thin pod from a tropical golden orchard; the tiny black seeds inside the bean imparts a luscious vanilla flavour.

extract obtained from vanilla beans infused in water; a non-alcoholic version of essence.

VINEGAR

balsamic made from the juice of Trebbiano grapes; is a deep, rich brown colour with a sweet and sour flavour. Originally from Modena, Italy, there are now many balsamic vinegars on the market; use the most expensive balsamic vinegars sparingly.

cider also known as apple cider vinegar; made from fermented apples.

red wine based on fermented red wine.

rice wine made from rice wine lees (sediment), salt and alcohol.

white wine made from white wine.

WATER CHESTNUTS resemble a chestnut in appearance, hence the English name. They are small brown tubers with a crisp, white, nutty-tasting flesh. Their crunchy texture is best experienced fresh; however, canned water chestnuts are more easily obtained and can be kept about a month, once opened, under refrigeration.

ZUCCHINI also known as courgette.

MEASURES

One Australian metric measuring cup holds approximately 250ml; one Australian metric tablespoon holds 20ml; one Australian metric teaspoon holds 5ml.

The difference between one country's measuring cups and another's is within a two- or three-teaspoon variance, and will not affect your cooking results. North America, New Zealand and the United Kingdom use a 15ml tablespoon.

All cup and spoon measurements are level. The most accurate way of measuring dry ingredients is to weigh them. When measuring liquids, use a clear glass or plastic jug with the metric markings.

We use large eggs with an average weight of 60g.

DRY MEASURES

METRIC	IMPERIAL
15g	½oz
30g	1oz
60g	2oz
90g	3oz
125g	4oz (¼lb)
155g	5oz
185g	6oz
220g	7oz
250g	8oz (½lb)
280g	9oz
315g	10oz
345g	11oz
375g	12oz (¾lb)
410g	13oz
440g	14oz
470g	15oz
500g	16oz (1lb)
750g	24oz (1½lb)
1kg	32oz (2lb)

LIQUID MEASURES

METRIC	IMPERIAL
30ml	1 fluid oz
60ml	2 fluid oz
100ml	3 fluid oz
125ml	4 fluid oz
150ml	5 fluid oz (¼ pint/1 gill)
190ml	6 fluid oz
250ml	8 fluid oz
300ml	10 fluid oz (½ pint)
500ml	16 fluid oz
600ml	20 fluid oz (1 pint)
1000ml (1 litre)	1¾ pints

LENGTH MEASURES

METRIC	IMPERIAL
3mm	⅛ in
6mm	¼in
1cm	½in
2cm	¾in
2.5cm	1in
5cm	2in
6cm	2½in
8cm	3in
10cm	4in
13cm	5in
15cm	6in
18cm	7in
20cm	8in
23cm	9in
25cm	10in
28cm	11in
30cm	12in (1ft)

OVEN TEMPERATURES

These oven temperatures are only a guide for conventional ovens. For fan-forced ovens, check the manufacturer's manual.

	°C (CELSIUS)	°F (FAHRENHEIT)	GAS MARK
Very slow	120	250	½
Slow	150	275-300	1-2
Moderately slow	160	325	3
Moderate	180	350-375	4-5
Moderately hot	200	400	6
Hot	220	425-450	7-8
Very hot	240	475	9

CONVERSION CHART

INDEX

First published in 2008 by ACP Books, Sydney
Reprinted 2010.

ACP Books are published by ACP Magazines
a division of PBL Media Pty Limited

ACP BOOKS

General manager Christine Whiston
Editor-in-chief Susan Tomnay
Creative director & designer Hieu Chi Nguyen
Art director Hannah Blackmore
Senior editor Wendy Bryant
Food director Pamela Clark
Sales & rights director Brian Cearnes
Marketing manager Bridget Cody
Senior business analyst Rebecca Varela
Circulation manager Jama Mclean
Operations manager David Scotto
Production manager Victoria Jefferys

Published by ACP Books, a division of
ACP Magazines Ltd, 54 Park St, Sydney;
GPO Box 4088, Sydney, NSW 2001.
phone (02) 9282 8618; fax (02) 9267 9438.

acpbooks@acpmagazines.com.au;
www.acpbooks.com.au

Printed by Toppan Printing Co, China.

Australia Distributed by Network Services,
phone +61 2 9282 8777; fax +61 2 9264 3278;
networkweb@networkservicescompany.com.au
United Kingdom Distributed by Australian Consolidated
Press (UK), phone (01604) 642 200;
fax (01604) 642 300; books@acpuk.com
New Zealand Distributed by Netlink Distribution
Company, phone (9) 366 9966; ask@ndc.co.nz
South Africa Distributed by PSD Promotions,
phone (27 11) 392 6065/6/7; fax (27 11) 392 6079/80;
orders@psdprom.co.za
Canada Distributed by Publishers Group Canada
phone (800) 663 5714; fax (800) 565 3770;
service@raincoast.com

Family favourites: the Australian women's weekly /
food director Pamela Clark.
ISBN 978-1-86396-744-0
Notes: Includes index.
Subjects: Cookery.
Other Authors: Clark, Pamela.
Also Titled: Australian women's weekly.
Dewey Number: 641.5
© ACP Magazines Ltd 2008
ABN 18 053 273 546
This publication is copyright. No part of it may be
reproduced or transmitted in any form without the
written permission of the publishers.

Home economist Rebecca Squadrito
Nutritional information Belinda Farlow
Photographer Tanya Zouev
Stylist Vicki Liley
Food preparation Arianne Bradshaw
Cover Macaroni cheese with olives, page 62

The publishers would like to thank the following for
props used in photography: Maxwell & Williams,
The Essential Ingredient, Cloth.

Scanpan cookware is used in the AWW Test Kitchen.

To order books
phone 136 116 (within Australia) or
order online at www.acpbooks.com.au
Send recipe enquiries to:
recipeenquiries@acpmagazines.com.au